Welfare + Diversity:
Social Suicide

Carolyn Franklin M.A.

There are two steps to Social Suicide:

1. Welfare

"Free money" is an addiction; like any drug, the money and assistance are never enough. Society cannot support the exponential increase in the cost of welfare and especially an increase of babies born to single girls. This expenditure takes a heavy toll on monies needed for the elderly and ill. Also we "Haves" are unwittingly destroying the self esteem of welfare recipients by doling money instead of education and independence.

2. "Us" against "Them"

We are dividing people by labeling them "Hispanic," "African American" and "Native American." We are a nation of Us against Them. If we are a nation of "us" then why are these people identified as "other?" For America to survive, welfare must change, social divisions must end. This book provides the way.

Suicidal Socialism (or Suicidalism) is the downward spiral into extinction when a society, in its efforts to be good to its downtrodden and poor, consumes its own seed-corn, or regenerative resources. As in Rome, dictators offered citizens free bread and circuses. Venezuela, the dictator offered citizens free gasoline for their cars. In efforts to assuage their populations' increasing demands for "free stuff" resources are nationalized, and entrepreneurial activity is killed. It is the hammer of government regulation combined with the pruning sickle of initiative. The Russian Politburo under Brezhnev posted signs: "Initiative will be punished". Government by diktat lead to the downfall of the Soviet Union. The downfall of Venezuela and North Korea are inevitable. Margaret Thatcher said: "The trouble with Socialism is that pretty soon you run out of other people's money." (John Prince 2018)

Contents

SUICIDE 1

  1. WELFARE 3

  2. WELFARE IS ADDICTIVE 5

  3. DISADVANTAGED…defined............................... 7

  4. RETHINKING "DISADVANTAGED" 10

  5. THE GOOD OLD DAYS...................................... 12

  6. LIBERALS Liberal Logic 16

  7. AFFIRMATIVE ACTION 22

  8. IMMIGRANTS 25

  9. THE "LUCKY" WORKING CLASS 29

  10. SWEET CHARITY 32

  11. THE DISADVANTAGED NEXT DOOR 37

  12. APPALACHIA 43

  13. SINGLE WIVES WITH CHILDREN.................. 44

  14. IGNORANCE IS NOT BLISS - WHAT ABOUT "WHY"? 46

  15. CRIME 50

  16. THE INCREASE IN NEIGHBORHOOD CRIME.... 55

  17. THE CYCLE OF PIMPS, DRUGS, JAIL............. 57

  18. WELFARE RECIPIENTS PAY TAXES?............. 60

  19. MORE BABIES = MORE MONEY 62

  20. BROTHERHOOD - FAMILY 63

  21. CAPITALISTS 65

  22. SOUTH AFRICA 69

  23. EDUCATION IN AMERICA 73

  24. PREGNANCY IS A <u>CHOICE</u> 75

  25. FEMALES <u>DO NOT</u> "GET" PREGNANT 77

  26. ADVERTISEMENTS 80

  27. FOSTER CHILDREN 81

  28. TV PROGRAMS FOCUS ON EMPTY LIVES 82

  29. CHANGE THE CONCEPT OF "REWARD" 84

  30. JUDAISM   ISLAM 86

31. CHRISTIANITY 89
32. WHY UNIVERSAL HEALTH CARE WON'T WORK 91
33. PROVIDE BIRTH CONTROL 98
34. SAVE WELFARE PEOPLE FROM EXPECTATION OF FAILURE. 99
35. TWO-SIDED VIEW 102
36. CESAR CHAVEZ: "A Man Must Have Dignity" ... 103
37. AFTER THE FACT 106
38. ALL YOU WANT IS MONEY! 122
39. PEOPLE LEAVING AMERICA 123
40. THE HOMELESS 125
WHERE THE MONEY WILL COME FROM FOR THE PROGRAMS 127
FINALE 129
THE FISHERMAN AND HIS WIFE 130
THE GOOSE THAT LAYS THE GOLDEN EGGS 134
ABOUT THE AUTHOR 136
OTHER BOOKS BY CAROLYN FRANKLIN 137

SUICIDE

SUICIDE: "The act of taking one's own life voluntarily and intentionally." (Google)

The definition of suicide usually describes a single person taking his or her own life, to destroy one's self, usually due to feelings of helplessness and despair.

SOCIAL SUICIDE:

Where suicide is an intentional act for a single person to destroy his or her own life, "social" suicide is the intentional self-destruction of an entire society.

America is committing social suicide by spending substantial monies and energy to support a life-style of little education and unplanned population increase. The monies extended are considerable and there is no return on the investment.

Any investment in society should encourage an increase in a self-sustaining population; one that contributes a positive effect to society in general. Financial assistance should not result in a decline of self-determination and self-respect.

Welfare is not an investment - it's an expense. There is no "return" on welfare.

Division: By labeling parts of the population with artificial titles: "African American," "Hispanic" and "Native American," we have cut off a substantial portion of solidarity by seeing them as "other" - they are not "us" - they're different.

This separation encourages a substantial portion of the population to be recognized as a "minority," therefore "disadvantaged."

They're separated by the majority of Americans and understood as "different," helpless people who need the support and guidance of their successful peers. Yet who, in spite of being labeled "different," are expected to be regarded by the general public as the "same" as mainstream.

You cannot be mainstream and different simultaneously. An absurdity.

"A house divided against itself cannot stand."

1. WELFARE

In its current method of use, welfare supports and encourages some people to consider themselves as "worth-less." We "pay" people to decline into a cycle of no-education and no concern of the welfare of others. A substantial portion of the population are people paid to "do nothing," who have no value of self or others.

By supporting and defending the "do nothing" way of life we're symbolically killing the "Have-nots" by starving the drive, creativity, intelligence and healthy psychological development of a considerable segment of society. The "Haves", create a life-style which destroys the unique identity of self, of achievement in those people who take, but don't share.

The Haves are not only encouraging the psychological suicide of the Have-nots, they are participating in their own economic destruction. There is no pot of gold at the end of the rainbow. There is no interest return; money is finite.

For the good of all society, the Haves and the "Do-Gooders" need to re-evaluate welfare. What are the Do-gooders really doing that's good? Have they examined the current results of their uncommonly large generosity? What are their goals? Are they realistic? Is there any evidence the Have-nots have been lifted into a better way of life - of self-pride, independence, positive achievement and value?

Or, have they just increased in number, not in achievements?

Are the "Noblesse Oblige" supporting the perception of pity among the Have-nots - the "poor things"? Do the Noblesse Oblige have an ulterior reason to keep the "poor" from attaining a life of self-respect?

The Do-Gooders and the "Well-meaning" are not in the "Benevolent Business" to help the "Down-trodden"; perhaps they're in the Benevolent Business to get a gold ticket to heaven. A Do-gooder assumes pride knowing that she, or he, has a privileged life - they're "special," welfare recipients are "disadvantaged."

It's the story of the "Fisherman and His Wife." Will the ending for the United States of America be the same as it was for the fisherman's wife? She was never satisfied, ever wanting more, until her greed imploded - as it must in welfare.

2. WELFARE IS ADDICTIVE

Change is difficult for any addict. To "kick the habit" addicts become irrational; attempting to remove an addict from his drug of choice, welfare - "free" money - could result in an explosion, of anger and resentment.

The cost of welfare continually increases, but weaning disadvantaged people from their lifestyle may court a serious social backlash - a backlash of riots, protests, destruction of public buildings, small businesses and private property. The Haves seem unable to understand the cost to all of us for their halo of sainthood.

But the Do-Gooders must either anticipate and control the potential anger of the Have-nots, or risk the implosion of the Unites States of America.

Welfare is addictive from two points of view:

1. The Do-gooder is addicted to saint-hood, benevolence. There seems to be a compulsion to take care of someone so that the Do-gooder can control others, assume a god-like attitude of superiority. Perhaps he or she is empty of self-esteem and needs to help others as a sign of personal superiority, success…'?

2. Free money is hard to resist - like drugs. It's like the Benevolent Ones are the "pushers," suppliers, and the welfare recipients are hooked - the addicts. If the pushers were discouraged, there would be fewer addicts. But to have a society encouraged to snort taxpayers' income,

we all go down, not just the "addicts".

This book gives reasons, examples, facts, opinions as to how fast the USS America is sinking. It's critical that we change our system. However, changes must be based on education; society must understand that change is critical, change can be good.

When change is based on education, self-improvement, self-value, it's to *everyone's* advantage. We develop a healthy society.

3. DISADVANTAGED…defined

The concept "disadvantaged" is a catch-all phrase defined as: "unfavorable social or economic circumstances." (Google)

"Unfavorable social circumstances" is defined as: "disadvantaged, lacking social support." (Google)

"Unfavorable economic circumstances" is, "economically deprived." (Google)

There were about 15 children running wild on the ferryboat to Angel Island. They dashed up and down the stairs, zipped around the narrow walkway and pushed people aside to pass them. The majority of tourists that day were older people, frail tourists. There were no hand rails on the steps and the decks were slightly wet.

Apparently there was no one in charge. As I walked up the broad steps to the main deck some child shoved me aside and ran ahead. I yelled at him, "HEY! Cut that out!"

Immediately a young woman was at my side glaring at me, "You yelled at him - you need to apologize."

I was completely caught off-guard. "Apologize?" For getting shoved aside?

The woman explained to me, "These children are disadvantaged."

*I apologized, but later, I wondered why - I was **rewarding bad behavior!** I was teaching "dis-advantaged" children bad behavior was acceptable because they're lower income level.*

It took me some time to analyze that situation. Because

someone is defined as "disadvantaged" he's allowed to shove people, run amuck in a crowd of elderly people and, in general, behave without any consideration of the rights of others.

Why? Does this make ANY sense?

Apparently the children are experiencing "unfavorable social circumstances."

But, wait! Exactly WHO is experiencing "unfavorable social circumstances"? The children - or, the older adults who fall and break bones easily when they're pushed or shoved?

The children are creating their OWN unfavorable social circumstances. The children make themselves disliked, misunderstood and very unwelcome - then ultimately blame their situation on someone else - and, rightly so. They were taught, encouraged, to behave badly.

I was *deliberately* shoved; that bad behavior was rewarded, magnified, encouraged by a Do-gooder.

So, paradoxically, the disadvantaged are correct; their bad behavior *is not their fault! We have to "understand" it*...

That was an opportune moment to take the child aside, quietly explain the situation calmly and clearly, "You do not run in crowded areas, especially with older people maneuvering stairs with no railing. You do not shove people under any circumstances and you apologize if you accidentally bump into anyone."

The child should have apologized. That incident was an opportunity to teach someone that bad behavior is *not rewarded.*

One of my liberal friends was annoyed that I wanted to chastise the child. She said, "It's not the child's fault - he had bad parenting."

I was at a loss to understand her "logic." Her point of view is "after the fact." After you get shoved down a flight of stairs, it's too late to blame "bad parenting." Bad behavior needs to be addressed *immediately.*

It reminds me of a moment at a super market when two boys, in a hurry, dropped their bikes directly in front of the automatic doors and were about to rush inside.

I called out, "Boys, come back please." They did. I explained that someone coming out the doors would step on their bikes, fall and get injured - and may also wreck their bike.

That they understood! I suggested a safer place for the bikes, the boys moved them and went in the store. It was a teaching moment, easy, immediate and sincere.

What's wrong with that?

4. RETHINKING "DISADVANTAGED"

Liberals are well-meaning individuals who help disadvantaged people clean their yard by throwing the empty beer cans in the neighbor's yard, then are outraged because the neighbors object - the neighbors should "try to understand them."

By some twisted logic, Liberals seem to believe that to demonstrate social inequities by violence, smashing store windows and people's windshields - a Robin Hood approach - mainstream society will see the logic of their actions and rally to their cause - take from the "rich", i.e. middle class, and give to the poor.

That concept of logic baffles me. I was raised as a Yankee, in Massachusetts, at a time when people worked, paid for what they bought, kept their yard clean, were peaceful neighbors and proud to be American - somehow those habits seemed reasonable and right - and still do.

As an older adult, I was visiting "home;" life is slow in Massachusetts; change comes only when necessary, and that's hardly ever. I sat, on a lumpy old couch in the parlor at Uncle Carmen's flat. Carmen and Aunt Marguerite, both in their 80's, were philosophizing.

Uncle Carmen was sitting in the big overstuffed chair by the Zenith radio. A cigar draped, half burned, in his right hand; his left hand held a whiskey glass half full.

Aunt Marguerite sat in her old rocking chair… rocking back and forth … back and forth… staring, absentmindedly, out the window. Carmen was exasperated, "What I want to know is, why do people do the things they do!"

4. RETHINKING "DISADVANTAGED"

"Yes!" I thought. "That's what I want to know, too!"

Without moving her gaze from the lace curtains, Aunt Marguerite quietly said, "People do what they do because they want to."

Let me repeat:

*"People do what they do because **they want to.**"*

A simple, profound observation of human behavior.

I was stunned. Of course! Everyone has choices, right, wrong, good bad - we *choose* what we want to do. There is always a choice - first choice or not - *we have choices.*

I can hear the screech of anguish from the Liberals, "**NOT NECESSARILY!**"

Yes, we *do have choices*; we make choices every moment of every day! All too often when we make a poor choice we blame it on someone else.

The Law of Cause and Effect cannot be broken without serious backlash.

And society is a perfect scapegoat to blame for our problems; it's anonymous, broad, and anyone's opinion as to whom it includes. The inevitable backlash is "not my fault" - it's "theirs."

This eventuality is exactly why we need to encourage education. We Haves must teach the disadvantaged that they, too, have choices and consequences. Everyone must understand the advantages to society when each one of us contributes to his own improvement.

5. THE GOOD OLD DAYS

When I was a kid everyone I knew was either at work or in school. We wanted to achieve a good life for the sake of our family and America in general. We were Nationalists - as *ALL* countries are - not Isolationists, *Nationalists.*

As an aside, I am so disgusted with the "isms" and the "ists" that are subjectively plastered on anyone who disagrees with the speaker. The "ists" and "isms" are invalid, a desperate ploy to avoid honest disagreement, and hopefully, resolution. If someone doesn't agree with your position, suddenly you're an "ism," or an "ist."

Labels save the tedium of intelligent thinking.

No one threw garbage in their yards, left broken-down cars at the street, smashed windows or wrote offal graffiti in public areas. That was not the American way.

What happened since I was a kid and now?

Welfare happened.

Politically Correct happened

We must "understand them" happened.

Disadvantaged happened.

Smashing store windows happened - that is, select, high-end stores and neighborhood stores of hard-working locals!

Destruction of property could be the destruction due to the hatred, of self. Or a subconscious action to destroy the perceived differences in life-styles.

5. THE GOOD OLD DAYS

However, NO ONE in America is disadvantaged.

Imagine a neighborhood that has nice homes, manicured lawns, clean streets - no potholes, no broken glass, no graffiti. Just a serene setting for happy families and a pleasant atmosphere.

Every weekday the neighbors leave early for work at good jobs they have earned after years of school and training. They work, pay their bills, send the kids to school and the kids have after-school activities.

But, there's a hypothetical woman in that neighborhood who has a diverse life-style. Graffiti blares from the garage doors, fast food wrappers pile in her yard, crunched beer cans and cracked windows are statements of her *choice* of life style.

Her children knock over neighbors' garbage cans - they, themselves don't bother to put out cans for collection. They scratch the neighbors' cars with rocks and leave their toys on the sidewalk for people to trip over. Fathers stop by for a quick visit - a sort of a "Hi - where's your mother? I'll just be a minute."

"Ah, but," the Liberal says. "We mustn't judge her - she's disadvantaged."

What is the link between disadvantaged and picking up an empty beer can? How does lack of income discourage her from picking up food wrappers, and sweep up the broken glass from the smashed windows?

She's dispirited from the poverty she faces daily; what can she do - she's disadvantaged.

It's obvious even to the casual observer this woman has no intention of helping herself. Why should she when she doesn't have to? Who's going to force her to pick up her garbage, paint over her graffiti?

I read an article saying garbage at one's home is an indication of "demoralization." This is easy to understand; when someone is depressed or feels helpless, garbage in the street adds to the general malaise of the neighborhood. But, of course, the anti dote to this malaise is to clean up the area; lift up yourself, the appearance of a neighborhood, and you lift up the entire neighborhood; everyone's property increases in value and self esteem.

Liberal organizations will fight for her right to destroy the neighborhood - their message is that the neighborhood must understand her even if it reduces the quality of its life-style to accommodate this woman's rights.

The value of the neighborhood drops; the neighbors are forced to sell their home as cheaply as possible to move to a clean, safe area.

What happened to **their "rights"**?

In the story of "The Emperor's New Clothes," it's obvious the Emperor is naked, but no one wants to say so for fear of looking bad, or getting the powerful angry. To state the obvious is dangerous because someone has to stick his neck out, run the risk of being unpopular or look like they're not concerned for the poor - the disadvantaged.

Doing the right thing is discouraged.

Why? The "right thing" now is to keep your mouth shut or be censored - it's "groupthink."

Groupthink is characterized by a group of people who band together in a common interest or goal. They agree to agree on everything. There no opposition to ideas, cohesion is paramount, there is no dissension. The group, as long as they band together, cannot be defeated nor be split up.

There is no critical thinking; no concept analysis, just blind following - "If we all agree, it must be good."

This type of rule, guidance, governance, is dangerous and detrimental to everyone in society. They cannot or will not see a problem nor a solution to a problem. As far as groupthink goes, there is no problem. They stagnate.

Free speech is dead; politically correct (PC) rhetoric has crushed creativity, thinking and individual expression - and HONESTY! **ETHICS!** Gone.

6. LIBERALS Liberal Logic

Liberal logic is an oxymoron. It is apparent from the definitions in this book that the concepts "liberal" and "logic" are incompatible.

By dividing American society, we become Haves and Have Nots. Not only do we divide people, we single them out for labeling: Hispanic, African American, and Native American. These labels immediately shout, "These people are 'different;' they're not 'us'." Those people are further denigrated as disadvantaged…why?

To be accepted mainstream, they must also be viewed as: *AMERICANS* - citizens of the *UNITED* States of America - not as "them," but "us."

Liberals have specifically labeled these groups to discriminate specific persons we should not discriminate against, because we are all the same - the different ones are us - an example of Liberal logic.

This is a disguise to white-wash an entire population, lift up poor people by the belief that the wealthy and privileged are obliged to help those less fortunate. We view these groups as lesser beings, those who cannot help themselves. Rather than accept these people as equals, we cull them and code them so now they're acceptable, "These people are not us, but we want to be democratic; we'll label them, put them in a separate category, pat them on the head and move on. Now they're sanitized - they're us!

American Indians

I am part Indian, Osage, and proud of it. I was born an Indian and still am an Indian. I am also a "native" American. A native American is ANYONE *born here.*

If the title "Indian" is offensive to someone, then let that person use an alternative, Indigenous people. Or address them by their correct title: Navajo, Cherokee, Osage… We could honor each tribe by using its specific tribal identity.

Particularly offensive to me is the term, "the" Native American; that is pronounced as "thee" Native American, insinuating there is but one type of Indian with only one culture. I heard a *college instructor* telling her class:

"The" (mispronounced "thee"- only kind there is) Native Americans place their dead in a coffin and set them above the ground on a stand. "Thee" Native Americans hunt buffalo with a bow and arrow. They live in tents made of animal skins, and so on.…

The ignorance of this teaching is staggering. At this moment there are 562 tribes of indigenous peoples in America, many having disparate customs and languages. There is no "thee" American Indian.

It's particularly annoying when people of a specific culture don't even recognize their "own kind" and discriminate against them:

A student, an Iranian girl, had brown skin, long, black hair, and was about 5'3". She told me her problem; she appeared to be of Mexican heritage so the Mexican-American girls on campus assumed she was one of their group and wanted her to speak Spanish with them. In vain the Iranian girl told them she was not Hispanic. They said she was lying because she wanted to pass as a White person. The girls were rude and called her derogatory names. This is a demonstration of gross ignorance and an embarrassment to both communities. Stereotyping!

Mexican Americans

Liberals are teaching Mexicans to be ashamed of who they are - *Mexicans*. If this is not true, then why the name change? Why change their identity?

Why are we referring to Mexicans as "Hispanics?" If you were born in Mexico, then you're MEXICAN. The description, Hispanic, means someone born in Spain or of Spanish heritage. Spain is at least 400 years away from Mexico, just as England is 400 years from America - we're not "Anglos," English-American, we are American.

Well actually, we don't refer to Mexicans as Hispanics - we refer to them with the soubriquet du jour: *Chicanos, Latinos, Hispanic, Minority, Mexican-American.*

Mexico is a beautiful, ancient country, with a people whose heritage and customs go back thousands of years. They are a proud people and rightly so.

Think about the confusion of a Mexican when he comes to America. All his life he's been a Mexican, suddenly he's a Hispanic - what happened? Other countries call him a Mexican, his legal papers state "Mexican," but when he steps onto American soil, he's a Hispanic! Are we trying to code, coverup, focus on his being poor - assume he's poor, by "liberally" altering a heritage? Why?

In the college where I taught we had a professor from Spain - he is Spanish. The Administration listed him as Hispanic - he was annoyed. He said, "I am SPANISH, not Hispanic!" He's a victim to a blatant display of American ignorance.

Asians

By the way…why aren't Asians separated into groups with exotic names? Are they disadvantaged? What are the qualifications for "disadvantaged?" Who decided who is disadvantaged and who is not?

In my avid, voracious readings of just about anything, I have read several books on the history of China, which tracks their vast shipping trades at many parts of the world including North America in the 1700's.

The ships were huge to accommodate cargo, merchandise, men - and the comfort girls who had their own ship following behind. There were usually 3 of these ships that travelled together to the shores of Mexico, Africa and Italy. In Venice, Italy, there's a monument to the Chinese Muslim Admiral, Zheng He.

Well, you know how it is, yes, the men, sailors, had their own comfort girls, but the girls on shore were too hard to resist - beautiful women. Some of today's Mexicans appear to be Asian-influenced rather than Spanish…? What about the lovely Venetian women…? Perhaps a DNA study would be interesting…?

My mother was born in Naples. I recently had my DNA done - beside Osage Indian, I am part Chinese! I am absolutely delighted! Who assumes the right to label others?

Black Americans

Referring to people as African Americans is ludicrous as there is NO country called "Africa." Myself, I'd call them Americans.

A Black American self-published his documentary on Public Television in his search for his African roots. Like many

Americans, he apparently did not understand there is no country called "Africa."

In one scene, the American was riding in a train (in Egypt), seated facing two Egyptian men who were wearing their burnooses and long flowing white robes. All three men were engaged in conversation.

The American smiled and asked the two men, "How does it feel to be African?"

Puzzled, one man replied, "We're not Africans; we're Egyptians."

Thanks to the vacuous labeling by the Liberals, the American sat there silently, He had no clue as to what was just said.

Liberal sanctioning

It takes a lot of guts on the part of the Liberals to change a nation's identity! And the population of Mexicans, Indian tribes and Black Americans allow it! They don't understand that they are separated, segregated and allowed into society only when it pays off for mainstream society.

"Politically Correct" (PC) "improves" their identity; these groups have no idea of how they're being denigrated.

IT'S DAMNED INSULTING!

It just occurred to me, did anyone *ask* this population of minorities if they want their identity changed? Did anyone take a poll on who wanted to be Hispanic, "African" American or "Native" American?

Did this group of people agree with being different? Who told them they were not "us," but, "them?" Were they pleased with their new identity - the separation from mainstream Americans?

Minorities? Are you counting by abacus or your pinkies?

Just for the fun of it, I looked up the statistics of the "minorities" by Google.

United States of America Population   328 million   June 2018

Chinese	3 million	2010
Mexicans	58 million	2015
Blacks	47 million	2017
American Indians	5. 2 million	2010
Indo-Indians	3 million	2017

Does anyone know the cut-off point to qualify for a minority? As we all know, statistics can be loosey-goosey as far as accuracy is concerned. But, statistically the above data is an indication of population numbers in America since 2010.

7. AFFIRMATIVE ACTION

Let's look at the covert message of Affirmative Action.

The intention of Affirmative Action was to improve the status of the minority, that is: Black Americans, Mexican-Americans and American Indians. This was a federal regulation to ensure that discrimination against people who were in a minority group had fair access to employment opportunities.

A potential employer cannot refuse to hire a person on the basis of skin color or national heritage. This legislation has been augmented to include women, gays and other, self-described, minority groups.

The intention is fair and reasonable. For any employer to refuse to hire someone *qualified* for a position would be to work against the employer's own interests.

But the legislation does not include the word, "qualified", which opened the door to a can of worms. Theoretically anyone can apply for any job and expect to be hired. The wording of the Action says the employee should train the minority for the job.

That can't happen; employers run a business, not a pre-school.

Therefore the covert message to a potential employer is:

> "You have to hire (insert minority) whether he or she is qualified or not. And, you may have to train them while you're paying them."

The result has been that the minority may or may not work out in the job. Even with tutoring and training some people don't always have the required basic skills. Because they lack those basic skills, employers are concerned that some potential workers will not always do a good job.

This failure to manage a job and ensuing rejection affirms to the minority that he

or she really is not hirable, a further humiliation. It would appear that even with laws forcing employers to hire them, minorities still can't do the job. Their seeming inadequacy is magnified.

The Affirmative Action was not thought out well; it meant well, but bungled. Whoever authorized it was not adequately versed in human nature. Perhaps they are well-versed in expediency - covering a problem with good intentions, but little substance.

The *intelligent* thing to do is to provide intensive *schooling, education, internships, counseling, guidance, encouragement, hands-on demonstrations, tutoring,* to bring *all* candidates up to standards - ***there are no short cuts.*** Bring each and every person up to speed; give them whatever assistance is needed to develop their skills so they can honestly say they have earned all they have.

I had one student, a woman about 40 years old who was very enthusiastic, loved giving speeches and was a lot of fun in class. I tried to guide her into the class content and gently coach her as she was not up to standard on understanding the class requirements.

Her major speech, the Persuasion Speech, was far short of the correct structure. I made a great many allowances for her. She was trying so hard to do well.

When she gave her presentation, she was so happy; as the speech progressed she began to understand it wasn't like the other students' speeches.

She stopped talking, laughed and said, "I'm so ghetto!"

She left class and I never saw her again.

That hurt my feelings. She was a wonderful person but had never been exposed to formal education. Without preparation she came directly into the ivy halls of Academia. So unfortunate.

*Another student, a young man about 20 years old, evidently had either no, or very little exposure to mainstream communication styles, i.e. **words**. It seemed he literally had no words!*

When he gave his Persuasion speech, instead of "talking" he used physical motions, waving his arms, using finger gestures, patting the sides of his leg, shoulders and his chest. He used eye movements and tipped his head.

It was fascinating but very little mainstream, communication. Also it was apparent he was terrified. After that speech, I never saw him again. I wanted so much to tutor him, but there was no opportunity.

Affirmative Action seeks to skip over the obvious - education - training; short cuts shoving a candidate into a job, don't work. Emphasis must be on current primary and secondary schools to set standards and *meet them.* To avoid stigma, these "catch-up" schools could have a uplifting name, "Opportunity University", some name that would also include retired people wanting extra education - anyone could go there for more training in many fields - free!

As a student, I applied for a part-time opening for an on-campus job disseminating information concerning campus activities, class locations and general information.

I qualified for the job. I was told they would like to have me, but had to hire a minority. They had hired several, none of whom worked out; but they had no choice, they had to hire another minority. Full circle. No one wins here..

8. IMMIGRANTS

Oh, I spoke too soon; yes, there are disadvantaged people in America. These are the thousands of immigrants who come to America from war-torn countries. They are desperate to escape starvation, imprisonment, violent crime and poverty.

They don't speak our language well and have no employment in sight- how do they survive?

They survive because they have Hope and Determination - a *willingness to work, and, they have PRIDE!*

I've met many of these immigrants in my classes. After stepping on American soil, as soon as they can, they go to school, learn the language, take any work they can get to take care of their family. Most of them have 2, 3 jobs at a time, to provide for housing, food, and - the most important to them, *education.*

One student, a man who escaped from Viet Nam by boat with his family, was so desperate to get to America the family paid any price - a ransom, to get to safety.

A pirate boat attacked them, took their money and valuables, ripped the gold teeth out of mouths, pulled some girls into their boat and left.

Then the pirates riddled the people's boat with bullets to destroy them. They were terrified. The boat was sinking fast, no land in sight. They bailed water with their hands - used anything they could find to save themselves. They had no food, no water, and even went without sleep to stay alive.

A storm came up, high winds. A huge wave picked the boat up (at this point my student cupped his hand sideways to show us how big the wave was) carried the boat forward and slammed it down on the shore of some island.

The natives on that island were not friendly; the boat people were imprisoned for two years. Then, by another miracle, they were released to Australia temporarily. Eventually the boat people were shipped to America. (thank God!)

This particular student attended a night class of mine; he came early after work so I could help with his English; after class he asked for more help. I was grateful to be of service.

Another student, an older family man from China, told of how his family was starving. He stood up front talking while the class followed his escape from China to America; we were all spellbound.

He spoke quietly, slowly. His eyes reflected on his past, reliving the nightmare that brought him and his family on the torturous path, to safety in America.

"There was very little food - not enough for all the family. So we'd have a family council and make a decision as to who to let die.

He explained, you have only one Mother and Father, so you can't let them die. But you have children - you can always have more children."

So they would decide on which child to let die. Then they took one of the younger children out to a field, set the child on a rock and left it there to die of starvation.

(Even as I sit here writing this, the tears stream down my face. I am embarrassed by the privilege and abundance we Americans - *ALL Americans*, have. I had to stop him in his story as it was too hard for the class to listen to. I thank God for getting him and his family to safety in America.)

Another student of mine, a young girl from Mexico, D.F. was the 4th daughter of seven girls. All nine of the family lived in a piano crate outside of the city. Her father rented a cab and drove passengers to support the family.

The girl announced to her mother, "I am going to America, to my Aunt's house in San Jose (California), go to school and get a job."

The mother flatly refused. "NO! You will stay here and get married!"

This went on for awhile. Eventually, the girl left Mexico, went to San Jose, got a job nights at the YMCA, went to school days, learned the language, got her A.A. She started her own business cleaning houses, got married, bought her father his own cab and built a home for her family in Mexico!

If a young girl, not knowing the language, can get a job *and* get an education - *on her own* - why can't the *people born here*, who speak the language, can read and write the language - not be successful?

Well, about now someone will look at me sadly and say. "You don't understand."

I... don't understand...? Maybe that person doesn't understand! Maybe he or she is piling up points for sainthood.

Cadet Alix Idrache had tears of gratitude streaming down his face at his graduation from West Point Military Academy. Idrache is from Haiti, one of the poorest countries in the world. His heart was full of gratitude to America for the opportunity to become a stellar student and American citizen - America, the land of endless opportunities to become an outstanding person.

Alix didn't let the label "poor" deter him. His determination to rise above poverty, lift up himself, his family and his country, culminated in his graduation as a top student, in one of the best schools in the greatest country, West Point Military Academy. He, achieved all this on his own merit, his own drive.

By American labeling, this young man was disadvantaged, a poor thing. He could have stayed in Haiti, lost in poverty; facing a hopeless, empty future. But *he chose* to live a life of pride, achievement - he did all the work; he built himself up as an example of what is possible.

Why can't Americans, who have *every opportunity* for a better life, who can get help to lift themselves up, have access to education, who speak the language and already fit in - why would they prefer to be "down trodden" instead of "uplifted"? Why do some people choose pity instead of pride?

Why? Because we the Do-gooders, the Haves, the Saints, the Holier Than Thou's, need someone to be better than; someone we can cluck our tongues about the "poor things," then leap on our polo ponies and trot off for the big match.

9. THE "LUCKY" WORKING CLASS

A friend was out of work and we were discussing where she might apply for a job. She insisted her work was as a "Manager." When I asked, "Manager of what?" There was no "what" - she was a "manager."

I was confused. I assumed she had a specific skill of which she became proficient enough to be a manager. No. She didn't want the trouble of being proficient, she wanted the title and salary of whatever was available.

As we sat, drinking tea in my lovely home, wistfully she said, "You're so lucky!"

I snapped at her - lucky...? I'm LUCKY? I've been years in school, held down three jobs simultaneously to support me and my girls. I have a mortgage, insurance bills, IRS bills, orthodontist, water bill, gas bill, assessments, etc., etc. Oh, YES! I'm lucky!

She saw herself as disadvantaged; she had no job, no income, no ranch house. But all she had to do to get a ranch house, was get a job she hated, work 8 - 10 hours a day, at 2/3 the pay a man got for the same work, pay relentless bills and she, too, could be "successful."

Ah, but here's the rub, if people such as you and I, educated, financially stable, attends a religious organization, a benevolent organization, if we have no one to look down on, how then can we be magnanimous? How can we smile sweetly and feel good about donating time and money to the "less fortunate?" How can we lift ourselves up if there's no one to "put down?"

The first time I saw a man on the street holding a cardboard sign that said, "OUT OF WORK; NEED HELP," I felt so bad for him! The poor man needs help! I parked my car, rushed back and handed him a twenty dollar bill. Boy! I felt SO good! I had made a serious effort to bring a ray of happiness to someone's life!

The following day at my bank I mentioned to the teller how I helped the poor man who held up the sign. The teller told me he had an account at that same branch and came in with a handful of twenties every day!

I was cured from cardboard signs.

The priest at my church always made an effort to help people suffering from a hardship or financial emergency. He had a discretionary fund on hand to help people right then, no paperwork, no wait-time.

Two men at my church came to California because they heard the welfare was higher than in Arkansas. After signing up in California, each man received a monthly amount and several hundred dollars in "back pay". They were overjoyed! These disadvantaged men got an allowance for food, gasoline, phone bill, rent and free medical care. One man immediately signed up with a psychiatrist (free) for a sex change and got as far as medium size breasts when he died of an overdose of something - a drug he took at random from a friend's medicine cabinet.

Beside all the government hand-outs, our church gave them a monthly stipend to help them even more.

Then, our priest retired and a new priest took over. He was sharp, business-savvy and a strong leader. The two men went to him for continued help. The priest said, "Fine, bring me all your receipts, a list of all your income and all your expenses and we'll work out wha you need."

They said nothing, left, and never asked again.

Perhaps you may believe these are isolated cases. I wish they were.

10. SWEET CHARITY

Since churches have established their a reputation as a refuge, a rock on which to cling in times of trouble, they should designate a physical space to help the poor with tangible aid, rather than just rhetoric; instead of focusing on custom drapes, name brand sound equipment, manicured lawns, spacious auditoriums, gyms, interoffice phones and carpeting, simple living quarters could be set over the car port or on the grounds.

These dwellings would not detract from the elegant manicured lawns and park area surrounding the main buildings. Certainly the appearance of an organization helps bring in members and benefits from their free-will donations. "Curb appeal" goes a long way in attracting the right kind of members.

These nonprofit organizations could have emergency living quarters for the homeless and the battered wives on the property site. The organization could provide, temporarily, a small apartment for a family in distress, for people who are homeless due to misfortune and a place of safety for distressed teenagers.

The church I attended had a battered women's refuge on site - it was always locked and no one ever there to open the door. But the refuge looked good on the website. I don't think it was used once; people were referred to Social Services.

When I was in college, one of my classmates, also, a single working mother, was holding down part time jobs to support herself and her two children. It was close to Christmas and she was worried; she couldn't afford gifts for her children.

For the past two years I had been attending a certain church and they had a gift drive so needy children could get Christmas presents. I told my friend, "I'll get gifts from my church - they have lots of them piled up in the narthex."

At the church I explained to an Important Person the situation and asked for gifts.

They denied me!! I was shocked! They said something about the gifts were ear-marked for some special center. I could not have any.

*I waited 'til no one was looking and I **stole** four gifts, threw them in my car and took off! Ho, Ho, Ho! So much for Charity!!*

Churches and other charities **_pay no property tax_** (imagine!) You and I pay for their share of schools, police and fire protection, paved roads, street lights, libraries and parks. Not only do we pay out of our pocket to cover *their* city costs, but we lose considerable income from the wasted use of their land. Instead of parking areas for "private" religious clubs, and numerous brotherhood clubs, we could build income property so the capitalists could collect rent - i.e., income offset for taxpayers! *Socialism!*

I do not, <u>do not</u>, advocate socialism. I advocate intelligent capitalism; freedom to create, express one's self, achieve, but not to monopolize industry or labor.

Have you ever taken a moment to look at the grounds of most churches, synagogues, mosques, wards and temples? They're spacious, pristine and off-limits to non-members. Sometime, for fun, go to the front door of one of these sanctuaries during a service and observe how welcome you are. In some of them, notice how vigilante guards block you from entering.

They won't let you in, but they'll gladly take your tax money. (One non-profit church requires members to submit their income tax forms to that organization. That way the non-profit can be assured the member is tithing his full share.)

You are welcome at most Protestant, or Christian churches, but there are prominent "Christian" organizations that "wear a beard". Behind the beard these organizations are based on pressured donations ("dues") and blind obedience of members - they have no intention of assisting *non-members* - some of these organizations are often referred to as "cults"; *they are not non-profit.* These cults resemble private schools for specific members.

There is a very large church in my neighborhood with considerable surrounding property. The church plans to build a high-end shopping center on the property! Of course the shop rentals will be "non" profit! The message of this enterprise staggers my mind! Is this capitalism?

The "charities" win; the taxpayer loses. And the worst part is, some of the charities are not ones I would support under any condition. So my tax money is completely wasted. Very annoying!

The Baby Jesus was not "poor."

At times, during the Christmas season, when relating the circumstances of the baby Jesus' birth, narraters will emphasis how "poor" Jesus was. At the women's jail in Milpitas I often spoke on the misconception that Jesus was poor - most of the Christmas carols extol the virtue of being laid on a bale of hay among sundry farm animals.

Poverty is a condition of godliness, disadvantage that is easily overcome.

Because most of the women in the jail came from underprivileged families, low income, the wording of these hymns is erroneous, misleading for them. The covert message is,

"Jesus was poor, therefore poverty is a respectable state of life." In other words, "It's ok to be poor. You don't need to strive for success."

Here are the facts of the story. Joseph was a self-employed carpenter. He had his own business, very successful. He and Mary had to go to Bethlehem to be counted in the population data so their names would be on the tax records. Joseph paid taxes; he had an income and, I'd expect, savings.

Joseph was a capitalist, a business man, and a good father as we're told.

When they were on their trip, Mary was in an advanced state of pregnancy; so Joseph, being a good husband and prosperous, had Mary ride on a donkey. She didn't have to walk. Joseph could afford the luxury of having her ride for the trip. (I imagine being in an advanced state of pregnancy riding on a donkey was anything but comfortable!)

When they got to town, no hotel rooms were available; everything was rented. What to do? Joseph probably asked at the inns if anything, anywhere, was available - his wife was very pregnant and they needed a place as soon as possible! Understandably Joseph was worried - maybe frantic.

An inn keeper may have said, "Well, there's the stable; it's not much, but it's out of the cold..." And, Joseph, being concerned for his wife's comfort, took her there immediately and made her a bed the best he could out of the straw. This was not what he had in mind and, I imagine, he was not too pleased about the situation.

Then, the baby was born; the angels appeared to the shepherds; the Three Kings came along, all of them meeting in the stable.

What is the covert message here? My interpretation is that it's not about poverty. The facts would indicate just the opposite.

Imagine you're standing in an open space out in a field that has a roof over it - a roof just big enough to keep off rain. There's an open space where animals wander around, bumping each other, bleating and stepping on your foot. You see a strange crowd of people, barefoot shepherds, unwashed, wearing smelly fleece, standing next to kings wearing furs, capes, robes and bearing expensive gifts.

You might think, "Here we are, all standing together, side by side. No one seems to care how we're dressed or if we have gifts or not; we're all accepted."

The message is, "We're equal; everyone has a place in this world."

No one at that manger was un-employed; no one was jockeying for a better position. Poverty was not an issue; respect for all was paramount.

(This would not have happened at the Bethlehem Hilton with a "Do not disturb" sign on the door. The manger was a symbol of accessibility for all.)

11. THE DISADVANTAGED NEXT DOOR

I bought a four-unit apartment house in a lower income neighborhood. At that time I believed everyone was the same, everyone is just like me - what could possibly be a problem? People pay their rent, kids go to school and adults go to work. Renters live quietly and respect your property.

Partly true. Of my 3 tenants, 2 sets were very good. But, one set paid me with rubber checks and I had to evict them. They took it rather badly and destroyed some of my property - smashed in a garage wall. Their attitude was that I was rich and they weren't so they'd bring me down to their level.

The reality was I was working full time and paying off the mortgage. It was a financial struggle, but it was an investment for my children. It was all I had.

One other set of tenants had visiting relatives who were extremely difficult. I told those tenants their relatives' bad behavior was not acceptable - they couldn't come back on the property. My tenants readily accepted my decision; they were very afraid of those relatives, too, and I took a load off their minds.

It was kind of amusing. One of the relatives was the mother-in-law. She met with me privately to say their "bad" behavior was the way they did things in her country, implying that she had a right to do what she wanted here in America.

*I said, "This is NOT YOUR country, this is MY country, and this is MY apartment house. You **WILL NOT** behave that way in **MY** house."*

They didn't give me a second's trouble after that. Which affirms my theory, if you tell people you will NOT accept bad behavior, and mean it, the behavior will change.

Many people who have no property or investments as a life-line to provide for their families, would say I have no right to tell others how to live, no right to interfere in family matters. They say I should respect the customs of those people.

What about *my rights?* I would tell the critics that *they have no right* to tell me how to run my apartment house - *no right* to tell me who I can inhibit from beating up my tenants, from throwing garbage on the property. People who tell you that you have no right to do something, have *no right to tell you not to do something!*

This "browbeating" by people who are divested of your problems is vacuous.

In the neighborhood I could have put up with the daily errant problems, i.e., the neighbor's roof on fire from fire crackers, dead birds and my dead pet kitty from pellet guns, cars with loud engines roaring down the street, stolen flower pots, but after the knife-fight on my lawn early one morning - I drew the line. That was not my tenants - they, also were distressed.

I want to add a note about one of my tenants. I'm very proud of our relationship. She was a young mother at that time and I had "rescued" her from a beating by her husband's brothers. It was at 11:30 one night, her 6 year old son was banging on my apartment door to help them.

I dashed over, grabbed a man by his collar, told my daughter to phone the police and all 3 men were put in jail. I told my tenant and her husband that I would not allow this to happen in my home! I was very clear about it. From that day on she viewed me as her best friend - couldn't do enough for me! I really liked her and her husband. They were now freed from traditions of drunks and violence.

Overall, the neighborhood was not a pleasant place to live. I sold the apartment house and moved into a middle class neighborhood in a single-family home.

When I moved to the middle class area no one there was on welfare; no one was disadvantaged. The neighborhood was clean, quiet and safe - *a choice of life style.*

I say I have **every right** not to allow knife fights on my lawn, in my neighborhood. I don't need to "understand" these people - *they need to change!*

I have **every right** to insist on a safe neighborhood - for everyone!

Everyone has "the right of the pursuit of happiness." If you "pursue" knife fights, then move to another location - not in my neighborhood.

There seems to be a covert understanding that if you're on welfare, it's acceptable to turn neighborhoods into substandard housing areas. In fact, it seems to be expected that welfare residents will reduce property values and create neighborhood flight of concerned residents.

In my apartment neighborhood we all had dumpsters; these are very large metal containers for refuse - garbage. At my units the tenants put their trash inside the dumpster. They parked in their spaces, the driveway was always clean and the plants (that weren't stolen) were cared for.

But, in the apartment house next door to mine, the tenants threw their trash on the ground next to the dumpster. The trash was piled 6' high inviting rodents and emitted a pervasive stench.

I called the City Health Department, the apartment owner was notified and in a couple of days it was cleaned up - until the following week, same thing. We repeated this scenario for a couple of months and the problem was eventually corrected.

And, therein lies the difference between me and the Haves, the Candidates for Sainthood. I will *tell* people to pick up, clean up trash and maintain a health standard for everyone. *I will not do it for them.* Cleaning up your own trash is not a hardship - it is an obligation to the neighborhood.

Everyone must take responsibility for his actions. If he doesn't know what his responsibility is, *I'll tell him.* It's the obligation, the duty of every American to refuse to allow substandard housing and substandard neighborhoods - for their own sake! You see, *I do* understand them!

To this day, I fail to see the relationship between filth and poverty. How does being disadvantaged stop someone from putting a bag of garbage in its container? Does this happen because of laziness, indifference or ignorance?

Or, is it because we Haves, who have every advantage, encourage others to live in unacceptable conditions, because we perceive *them* as unacceptable? If we clean up the neighborhood, are we Haves implying that now the Have-nots are as good as we are? Are we Haves so bereft of self esteem our perception of Self has to ride on the shoulders of those less fortunate?

This led me to believe that if people are *told* some behavior is not acceptable - and you mean it, the unacceptable behavior stops. To enlarge on this, if you tell people there are consequences for bad behavior, and mean it - follow through, the unacceptable behavior at least gets modified if not substantially changed.

At any rate, people are on notice.

In general we are responsible for our own actions. No one makes anyone throw garbage on the ground - they do it because they don't know any better or they just want to, or they disrespect them-selves. After all, they live there; if the neighborhood is a garbage dump, then that's how other people see them and how they see themselves.

That's a *choice of life-styles.*

As Americans we are obligated to lift everyone up to ensure pride in our self and pride in our neighborhood.

> *On the news in some city, (New York?) a young man was trying verbally and physically to defend himself. He was surrounded by an angry mob, all yelling at once, waving arms, pumping their fists into the air; and, in general, terrifying him. It seems the young man had purchased an apartment house for income, and assumed that people were honest, respected other's property and cared about their own living area.*

Like me, he was so wrong.

In his apartment house the tenants were yelling about plugged toilets running over, garbage piled around the heels of passersby, smashed windows and scatological graffiti painted on the walls (by the way, what is the psychological symbolism of "blocked toilets" ?). The scene was disgusting.

The tenants wanted the place cleaned up and fixed. Rightly so. However, the tenants, themselves, had reduced the property to this state. They had no sense of cause and effect - the apartment was unlivable; they wanted someone else to clean it so they could continue to live in it and disrespect it. They were disadvantaged, on welfare - poor people.

The young man was surrounded by police; he stood in shock; the lack of logic, the total absence of conscience, of responsibility, of any understanding of right and wrong, was a concept and a way of life he could not process.

No one, other than the officers, defended him - everyone was afraid - afraid of censorship from the Haves, the Liberals - and, the mob was downright dangerous!

No one cared about the young man, his terror, his suffering; no one stood up for him - the taxpayer! - against the vacuous, vicious mob that surrounded him, waving fists, pumping their arms and yelling full force - he was terrified.

So, the disadvantaged prevailed, were rewarded - so disappointing and non productive. This behavior drags us all down - we are all "disadvantaged."

And we're told by the Liberals, we "need to understand them." Oh, *I do*!

12. APPALACHIA

When your work shuts down - your livelihood is pulled out from under you, then you have no choice - you *are* desperate, disadvantaged. This sad situation is not a choice of the workers. It's a national catastrophe.

When the mines were shut down in the Blue Ridge Mountains of Virginia, Kentucky, West Virginia, the entire work force in those states was shut down. The workers lost their present and their future - their lives stopped; they were at a standstill - a dead end.

We don't use coal any more; we don't mine any more as an occupation- thank God. That was a dangerous, dirty job that caused the death of thousands of workers over the years.

Those people are out of work, out of money and not by their choice. They would rather work - *want to work* - to support their families. Those people have pride in what they do and who they are. *Welfare is not their choice of life style.*

Those people are not disadvantaged - they're desperate. They deserve all the help they need. They have not "worked" the system; they have paid their share into the system. The country has let them down; we must honor them and give them what help they need - *now;* they have *earned* it.

They need substantial help in many ways. The help given them is not wasted; they had jobs and lost them - for them charity was not a lifestyle. But much of the money they could have used was sent to pay for babies born with no regard as to the family situation, no father available, no education in the home and no real home life. We took money, taxes, from the miners to reward other people who have no understanding of self pride and achievement as the miners do.

13. SINGLE WIVES WITH CHILDREN

There are no statistics on this category of poor people. This is a "lost" category of "single wives with children" - women who are the sole support of their family.

These women are married by definition, but have no husband or father with them. Their husbands are men who have decided married life is not for them; they've ridden off into the sunset with a young blonde on the back of their motorcycle.

Most of the mothers work to some degree. But it's hard to keep a job because one of the kids has a cold and can't go to school. She can't afford a sitter so she has to stay home and take care of the sick child. She makes a "woman's" wages, 2/3 of what a man makes for the same work, but she can't meet her bills on that amount.

Yes, she makes 2/3 of a man's wage, but she pays 100% of the cost of rent, a quart of milk, a loaf of bread… In actuality, she probably makes 1/2 of what a man makes.

She did not get pregnant irresponsibly. She had planned on a life with her husband and children; the same sweet dream of all new wives. But the rug was pulled out from under her.

And then you have an army of battered women who have escaped from the tyranny of abuse. Their marriages, also, have ended through no fault of their own. They have very little opportunity to work and also care for the children.

Incidentally, those of you who are innocent enough to think deserted wives get child support, well I pause in my writing to have a raucous laugh at your expense. *Very few* fathers pay child support. You can't maintain a blonde and a motorcycle on nothing! He needs his income for himself - well, he'd help - if he could…

There are laws to recover unpaid child support if you can locate the father. Or you can have him put in jail for non-payment of child support. But, what good is a father in jail? He's still not supporting his children - we are.

These overburdened mothers need all the help they can get.

They are truly disadvantaged.

14. IGNORANCE IS NOT BLISS - WHAT ABOUT "WHY"?

Unless it is understood by the public that "bad" behavior is not acceptable, bad behavior will not stop - it just gets more so - especially when we *encourage* it by those people who sympathize and understand it instead of correcting it.

And, it's helpful to understand any problem in order to more easily correct it. We could solicit advice and guidance from the ones who need change so we can all cooperate on the best direction to move.

People in general ignore bad behavior because: It's not my problem, none of my business, kids will be kids, don't make waves, don't start anything - just leave people alone. Don't judge others until you walk in their moccasins; we don't know what troubles they have; we don't understand them; people are basically good…on and on.

It's all true; but we choose to stay ignorant of *why* it's all true.

Sociologists, social scientists, psychologists, criminologists study poverty, crime, dangerous neighborhoods and comprehensive varieties of groups of disadvantaged people in: Violence, muggings, rape, burglary, delinquency, vandalism, etc., etc.

You name it; they study it; we live it.

After years of collecting data, these erudite, dedicated scientists amass charts showing where crime is the highest, poverty is the highest, drug use highest, first response is highest. Their statistics also show the increasing cost of welfare relating to the increasing numbers of babies born to unmarried girls.

The statistics of social problems are pin-pointed, reams of data, probabilities, as to what happens, where it happens and even when it possibly/probably will happen.

Yes, "what," "when" and "where" are explained in reams of data proving "what"…but how about "WHY?" No one has yet offered a probability as to why crime is prevalent in certain areas and certain times. But the real question is, "Why not?" Criminals know there's a better way of life, but this one pays so much easier, do nothing, and get a check!

Brilliant!

Well, actually, the Haves don't care "why." If they knew why they could fix it; but numbers, stats, only to tell "what" and "where". "Why's" are subjective - messy, a Gordian knot requiring time, experience and intelligence to untangle and, perhaps a prophet to discern the cues.

If we don't change the status quo, then the Do-gooders can continue to relish their magnanimity and the under-privileged can continue to relish the negative attention focused on their staged, miserable, profitable, sans souci life-style.

On one program Dr. Phil had two car jackers, heavily disguised to protect their identity. These were two young men, almost boys by the sound of their voices. They were explaining their strategies to take your car out from under you as you sat in traffic or while parking.

The sound of their voices denoted confidence and expertise in their life style.

*One woman in the audience kept crying out, "But, whyeeee? Whyeeee?" The obvious answer to her "Why" was because **they wanted to!***

Stealing cars, even with you, the baby in the car seat and the pet dog hanging out the window, car jacking is quick, easy and profitable. There's no overhead, no bulky equipment needed, no air conditioned office to maintain, no IRS forms - so, "whyeeee" not?

These young men were obviously intelligent, energetic, blossoming capitalists.

And you wonder why, being raised on welfare - (their admission), they were not taught a more acceptable means of occupation. It's a shame for society to lose their extraordinary intellect and drive (no pun intended) in their inevitable incarceration. They were successful Capitalists.

The Liberals can continue to avoid the responsibility to fix a wide-spread social mess. They can put problems "under consideration" - study the problem, 'til later; social problems that are engorged in violence and entitlement can be studied - later. No one wants to be the bad guy - the Enforcer - a Light in the Darkness; it's social suicide to avert social suicide.

It's a lose - lose situation.

Ignorance rules.

And, yes, each one of us has *the right* and ***the duty*** to ourselves to clean up the mess that affects us all. And, yes, we have the right to tell other people how to live their lives - if that life style destroys the quality of my life, and, *your* life.

Prayers for "peace, love, understanding and acceptance," holding hands, burning candles, singing maudlin songs is fine, but positive action, uplifting others is far more effective and practical - and perhaps, tedious.

People on aide programs are not stupid; but the people who believe the concept of pity, "the poor things," "we have to help them - they can't help themselves" are still on the turnip truck or lost in space (the one between their ears).

15. CRIME

In general, sociologists, psychologists and social workers seem to agree that people on welfare have low self-esteem which can cause rage, violence, depression and may be manifest in crime. If you destroy the property of others, you essentially destroy them. The property represents the people you fear or envy - you can't destroy the people, but you can destroy what they prize - their identity.

Rage is expressed by the smashed windows, street litter, vandalism, assault, car-jacking, drive-by shootings, street hold-ups - crimes costing tax payers, and property owners considerable expenditure as well as personal trauma.

But, perhaps this rage is a manifestation of self-hatred? Perhaps this destruction is a symbol of self-hatred, a lashing out at their perception of self, of who they think they are? What message have we implanted in their minds as to how we Haves see them? Do they see a very different message from what we Do-gooders intend? Is there a mote in our eye?

We were sitting, having coffee and chatting in my living room. Autris was one of my closest friends, a black man, baritone opera singer, whose voice was so beautiful. We were joking, talking about our future dreams, his, in particular with his extraordinary gift.

"Autris," I started, bubbling over with anticipation. "If you could have anything you wanted, what would it be?" I was thinking it would be top billing at the "Met."

He thrust out his chocolate brown right arm and said, "I would have this turn white."

I was stunned! The passion of that response overwhelmed

me! In spite of his incredible talent, his youth and good looks - he would give it all up to be white!

What have we done to him?

The cost to the working middle class is exorbitant. We pay, pay, pay. We pay welfare to take care of people; we pay to clean up the damages on the streets, highways, city halls, school equipment damage, damage to parks, beaches; we pay for incarceration; we pay for legal representation; we pay for rehabilitation, we pay for medical care; we pay for police protection; we pay in cash, high insurance rates, taxes, high stress and fear - it never ends.

Liberals point out people who commit crimes are "lost;" they had a bad childhood, were misunderstood, mistreated, abused, tormented - well who hasn't been misunderstood, mistreated, abused in some way…? Turning to crime is not an option.

We, Americans, have allowed this to happen because of a need to feel sorry for the down trodden, the underdog. We need to feel superior to less successful beings. Money is not the answer.

Self respect and education is the answer.

Self respect comes from knowing that you have value, can do things, meet social criteria that dictates the current concept of success. Self respect comes from knowing you can meet anyone eye to eye, idea for idea, create valid arguments and have the positive attention of society at large.

Crime is growing and going to get worse. What incentive do law-breakers have to change? Jails are full; we let people out early for minor offenses. Three meals a day, medical care, gym workouts, companionship - all free. And, when they get out of prison, they get back on welfare! Hey! It's all good! At least the law-breakers are not fools…

Education - for everyone. The solution is so easy it makes me suspicious of what might be really going on under cover…? Perhaps graft? Political corruption? The desperate need for mainstream self aggrandizement ?

Not only would crime, depression and low self-esteem be affected by education, we could put that tax payer money to positive use for everyone's benefit - maybe health care, higher education - technical schools, for *everyone*…?

> *On the Judge Judy program a sister was suing her brother. He was 7 years younger. Their mother died from heroin addiction when the boy was 11 years old. He went to live with his grandmother and the sister moved to a "better" neighborhood with her father, and later went into the military.*
>
> *They didn't see each other for years, but the sister sent him a few thousand to pay for schooling. He didn't use it for school; he spent it at random. Now, in court, his sister wanted him to pay the money back.*
>
> *His argument was that it was all her fault his life made a bad turn. She left him in a "bad" neighborhood. He said in the dangerous neighborhood he had no choice of what to do. He was in and out of jail four times. He needed the money to pay fines and lawyers. He said she should have taken him into the better neighborhood with her father. He was ordered to pay back the money.*

I've said, "Everyone has a choice of what they do." - we know right from wrong.

This young man knew right from wrong. He said he was in a "bad neighborhood" - this assumes a moral judgment on his part. But he was in a situation where he was confused, lost - *he was a child* and needed firm guidance of how to understand the right thing to do and how to avoid the "wrong" kind of friends.

Maybe when his mother was dying from heroin someone from one of the many benevolent charities could have placed that child where he would have better friends, where he'd have a chance to improve his direction and outlook in life.

It was not the sister's place to take care of him- she was a child also. I had thought that the father should have taken the boy to live with him, but then I wonder if they had the same father…?

He was apparently abandoned by society. This is so wrong. No child should be abandoned and lost. Somehow, in the system there should be a meaningful way to, systematically, remove children at risk and put them where they're safe.

This includes the 11 year old child in the following anecdote. She was lost in the system; she was forgotten at home - lost among other siblings, not tracked by the school, and no one cared. Inexcusable.

When I was a college student taking psych classes we were assigned a kid from "Juvie" (Juvenal Hall) to befriend.

I drew an eleven year old girl who immediately asked me for a "ciggy butt". I told her I didn't smoke. She seemed surprised. We had lunch; she helped make the salad. She'd never had salad before and we set the table - she'd never set a table before. She was on her best behavior, really very nice.

During lunch I played classical music on the radio. She was confused by the completely different sounds than she was used to. I was pleased she actually listened.

After lunch we drove around the City, San Francisco. She was fearful during the ride as she thought I was "out of my turf" and we'd get in trouble. I explained I had no turf. She seemed very apprehensive at that; if I had no boundaries I could be in danger of trespass and be attacked.

I took her home to her apartment; she'd been gone 6 weeks but her mother wasn't there to greet her. There was no furniture in the apartment, only a few clothes thrown on the floor. Two small children were alone, wandering around aimlessly. At "Juvie" there had been a mix-up in the spelling of her last name and when I explained to the mother she'd been in Juvenal Hall due to the name mix-up, the Mother said, "Oh, I wondered where she was."

So much for maternal instinct. So much for the well-fare of an 11 year old child! I wondered what all her welfare money was spent on; I guess we'll never know… Yes, the last name was spelled incorrectly (the girl probably didn't know how to spell it and mis-led the authorities), but the address was correct and the phone number was correct.

This means having a method to track the children, knowing who they are, knowing their home life, their progress in school, health care - difficult to manage? Yes. Costly? Yes. Perhaps meet with resistance? Yes. It means more than lip service, yes? Yes.

But, isn't this what we're paying for? Isn't this what you do when you really care about the well-fare of children…??

I am strongly suggesting you read Dr. Ben Carson's book, "America the Beautiful. Rediscovering What Made This Nation Great." He speaks eloquently of the benefits of education and of his personal struggle to educate himself. He suggests that his success in Life is reachable to people who want to improve themselves - lift themselves out of darkness into the Light. The road to the Good Life is not easy for most of us, but well worth reaching for.

16. THE INCREASE IN NEIGHBORHOOD CRIME

Almost every day, on the news, a stolen bicycle from someone's yard; someone mugged walking home from the grocery store; car jacking, cars stolen, tires stolen off cars, broken car windows, computers taken from cars, trucks, trailers, drug dealers grouped nearby, equipment stolen from yards. Homes, offices and businesses burgled. Many, many armed robberies at 7/11's and other corner stores. Almost every day a bank robbery.

Then the person interviewed by the newscaster says, "It's never been like this before - we've never had trouble here - this is a peaceful neighborhood."

It's going to get worse.

Why? Because we Do-gooders have trained these law-breakers they "can't help themselves" - they are poor, live in bad neighborhoods, underprivileged, disadvantaged - and, *we must understand them.* - don't correct - *change* - conditions; just *understand them.*

They just need a *chance*…a "chance" to do what…?

Oh, I hear that so much, "You have to give them a chance." How much of a chance? How often of a chance? Who monitors the chance? Who decides what, when, where and rules of the chance? Who measures "chance?"

Have they never had a chance at all - in AMERICA…? NO chance? Hmmm, I doubt that! Define "chance."

The young people are taught to understand they'e not responsible for their crimes - society is. Society didn't give them a break.

They can't get a job because they have no education, no permanent address and no skills,

If they break the law and are caught, they get off the street, get a mild sentence, put in a place where they three free meals a day, hot showers, free representation, free medical care, sympathy from the Liberals…

Where's the punishment? That is not the answer to crime - *education is the answer; w*hat have they *learned*?

Where is the deterrent to stop committing crimes? They have no home as such, no room in the cellar or attic where they store Christmas decorations. There is no "home," maybe a mother on drugs, several siblings from various daddies - this is "home," as created by the Benevolent Ones, the Do-gooders.

17. THE CYCLE OF PIMPS, DRUGS, JAIL

I held church services at the Elmwood Jail for women in Milpitas, California. Usually about 20 - 30 girls came to the services; they were a mix of races and ethnicities. And, all of them very nice people. The inmates were always respectful. Their approach to me was candid, open and receptive - I really liked them.

These girls did not belong in jail - they belonged in school. Their "crimes" were prostitution, drugs, petty theft. Outside of theft, none of the crimes had victims.

Drugs hurt the person who is addicted to them and as far as prostitution goes, well, I suppose from time to time there are dissatisfied customers - but then they can take their business elsewhere.

And, can *anyone* give a rational reason why prostitution is illegal?

I'm waiting…

These women were honest, guileless and down-to-earth - my kind of people! In general, they had been raised on welfare, had no skills and no education. Their lives in jail were a dismal cycle of empty days, week after week, month after month. Society put no investment in time or education for these women.

What message did the Do-Gooders send to them? No one cared about their "rehab" - they were "worth-less". - empty days, empty people.

I wrote letters to the Warden, the County of Santa Clara and the Mayor offering to volunteer twice a week to teach classes. The inmates lacked basic skills in math, how to read a contract, reading comprehension, understand interest rates, establish a bank account, know how to pass a job interview, social skills, etc - all Communication skills - my field of expertise.

And, for FREE!!

I wrote on two occasions and never had the courtesy of a reply. What does that tell you about rehabilitation? What does that tell you about a serious program, a plan, to alleviate crime?

The common denominator of the group was their lack of formal education. They were trapped in a cycle of drugs, pregnancies, pimps and hopelessness. When released, they had nowhere to go but back into the same cycle of crime, incarceration and release. Think of that in terms of cost to the taxpayer, all lost money - no return either in psychological improvement for the women or tax relief for the county.

All of these girls were on welfare. Some of them wanted to bring their children to live in the jail with them. I understood their need - a mother wants her child with her; but jail is no place for children.

Why are people who have nothing, no job, no home, no income, no education, no hope, allowed to have children? How does this kind of life provide a healthy and loving place to raise a child?

We need to provide, encourage the use of, and, insist on, the use of birth control if there is no healthy, loving place to raise a child. People should not be encouraged to have children when they, themselves, have nothing to offer the child.

I have heard the Haves defend this lifestyle as, "Well, the mother loves the child and every child needs to be loved."

If you "love" your child, why do you *purposefully* bring it into a world where you have nothing to offer it?

That kind of thinking is vacuous. That kind of thinking is used by the mainstream to avoid taking the thankless task of helping these girls understand who they are, their abilities and their responsibility in raising a child. This investment in time and energy is colossal - no wonder mainstream Do-gooders chuck off the responsibility with platitudes!

The women/girls in jail had no concept of cause and effect. They could only understand one position - theirs. The fact that they were a negative force in society was not clear to them nor did they ever observe their impact on their personal life - their immediate environment. They were never told their life could be changed, never told how to leave this depressing cycle of drugs, pimps, babies and jail.

Years ago when I was in school we were required to read, "Love is Not Enough," Bruno Bettelheim. You might want to look into what his observations and conclusions were about disadvantaged children. At that time we Haves were absorbed in meaning well, singing about social reform, "Love Makes the World Go 'Round"…

But, Love, alone, is *not enough*. It takes education, understanding responsibility; doing the daily drudgery of listening, tracking lost souls, shoveling sand against the tide - it never ends.

18. WELFARE RECIPIENTS PAY TAXES?

There is on on-going myth that welfare recipients pay taxes - supposedly they are not just "takers," they pay taxes just like working people. That is a pathetic attempt to cover up the fact that again, welfare recipients contribute nothing tangible back into society - and that is not their fault - it's ours!

This concept is fostered to bolster the ego, perception of self. This propaganda is necessary as we don't want welfare people to realize they're being patronized - which even further reduces their self esteem.

They pay their fair share…? How? The exact process has been glossed over, the pea under the walnut shell game.

Tax money goes to pay the welfare recipients. So if they pay back in small part what we gave them in large part, how does that help the taxpayers? The money goes to the "capitalists". Welfare recipients are handing back a tiny fraction of what we have given them.

What are *they* paying?

The State of Oregon has no sales tax. Consequently the entire burden of financing state programs falls on the home owners. Property taxes are a heavy burden for the new home owners but more so for the old timers who see the rates going up for them and no return in their services.

A sales tax bill has been suggested to up the allocations for the schools and other much-needed programs, but the homeowners rejected it. They say they're over taxed as it is.

But if everyone had to pay a sales tax, it would mean each person would contribute some money for State programs. The property taxes may not decrease, but the funding allocations would be eased for the homeowners.

With a sales tax, everyone would be required to contribute some monies. And, the states of Washington and California would be forced to do their shopping at "home" for their own economy.

19. MORE BABIES = MORE MONEY

I was impressed with the double standard of welfare vs a working person when one of my female students mentioned how much money her pregnancy cost her. She is a single parent who lost money being home during her first weeks of child care, and, she also lost money having to pay for pre-natal care and delivery costs.

She had a part-time job to pay for her schooling. The baby cost her considerable income.

Conversely, a girl on welfare gets income continued during her pregnancy and all delivery costs are paid by the same working girl who lost income for the same reason - and, oh yes, the welfare recipient gets a child-care allowance for the next few years. Why work?

What's wrong with this picture?

20. BROTHERHOOD - FAMILY

According to interviews and data, welfare children, and others, in the neighborhood group together to form surrogate families. There may be people around, but the home is "empty", devoid of family unity. At home (their physical home) there's probably a mother, siblings and very likely a grandmother or a "play" mother.

A play mother is a woman who takes an interest in the child and helps him face the world the way she would her own child. She is usually a stable factor in the child's life - a positive support to simulate a loving family. (Every home should have a play mother.)

But too often, noticeably missing from the family circle is a father, a male image who models warmth, protection and group cohesion.

With no father present, an unstable mother and a voluntary, occasional, play mother as well as various siblings - who may not match in physical appearances, group together to form a family. Children sense when they're not wanted, not welcome, not loved.

Can you understand how that fills them with despair, a sense of helplessness, an emptiness in their heart that will never be filled?

Children intuitively, instinctively, seek protection and companionship - a "family." Since there is rarely a father in the welfare home, children seek male models of strength and caring; they form surrogate families, "gangs," that give them a sense of male support, the (fictional) father they long for. It's human nature to bond with a strong parent-figure - someone who loves you and takes a special interest in you.

These young men will never have a true leader, someone to look up to; someone who loves them - someone who sees only them, as being special. They are the residue of welfare, not puppy mills, but baby mills - so wrong.

I have read reports written by the evaluators of how happy the children are, how the families love each other, support each other - on and on raving about the warmth and caring in the welfare families.

If this is true, then why are there so many gangs that swear allegiance to themselves, take oaths of membership, stand together - create a family? If these young men are loved and nurtured at "home,", then why do they turn against society with such hatred and gratuitous violence?

And those of us who are the Do-gooders, the Right to Life, the Pro Life, send these young men to jail for participating in gang activities; we give them no leadership, no guidance, but send them to jail where they can perfect more violent behavior.

These young men don't go to school and have no interest in a job. They have time, empty time. As it says in Proverbs 16: 27 - 29: Idle hands are the devil's workshop.

Yes, we've given them "well - fare", but no love. So sad.

This breaks my heart.

21. CAPITALISTS

The prevailing rhetoric confuses me. So many people want to do away with capitalism. If we listen to the Liberals and destroy capitalism - then somehow the middle class - the workers, everyone, will be rich; no one will have to work!

What am I missing?

If we don't have capitalism, where will the money come from to give away? Isn't that what Hitler did in the '30's … destroy businesses so all of Germany could be wealthy? Kristallnacht?

Whenever I ask for intelligent answers I get disdainful looks as though I were insensitive - don't understand. I don't care about poor people. I get rhetoric - no answers - no intelligence.

Well, true! I don't understand - so *explain* it to me in *factual terms* - not emotion, not disdain. Some people seem to want all give-away programs - a come-and-grab program - perpetually instill a feeling of inadequacy in others, perpetually feed them a diet of "poor thing, not good enough, can't make it, need help, let me do it for you…"- a destructive message.

This way Liberals can be the "good guy", giving away someone else's money will raise their own esteem.

Often Capitalists are held responsible for the condition of the nation - they are why poor people exist. Capitalists are held responsible for people who smash windows and throw garbage in the street.

What is the link between people who deliberately destroy the property of others and Capitalists paying wages in return for producing a viable product? Exactly how do the Liberals plan on relieving Capitalists of their money - their initiative, their drive, their education, their ability to achieve, their years of schooling and their financial risk and their investment in the health of this nation in general…?

Let's go with the concept that Capitalists are greedy money mongers who exploit the poor - get rich on the backs of the poor. I assume these "poor" are those who are the working class…? Is this class not aware they can say, "No, thank you"? Don't they know they can turn down a job offer if the pay is too low, or even walk off the job for any reason - strike? Just open the door… walk out?

Don't they know they have the freedom and the representation to strike? Don't they know they can move to a socialist country, get off the boat, and, be rich?!

The working class is actually in charge! The Capitalist has no business, income, or stacks of gold coins without the working class!

But as long as you're on a "give-away program", you'll never amount to anything, always be poor, down-trodden and rejected.

We can create "work-away programs" - you earn your way. Build up self-pride, self-esteem, a feeling of worth, of value, know you're just as good, just as wonderful as anyone else.

Former President Barak Obama told the Capitalists, "You didn't make it on your own." No, of course not! *Obviously!*

Capitalism is a combination of people who work and people who think, create, have drive, organize, spend countless hours preparing an 8 hour job so someone else can, also, have a home and security.

So, WHY are people disadvantaged? Because they have:

No education? Education is FREE in America.

No jobs? Look in local store windows, many "Help wanted" signs are prominently displayed.

They are down-trodden, in despair, have low self esteem, bad childhood…? So, who doesn't?

Too ill, mentally disturbed, special needs? Then put these people in an institution where they STAY and get all the care and help they need.

Like the two men who drove from Arkansas to California because the "pay" (welfare) was better in California. They actually had a car for the trip, bought gas, lodgings and food for four days.

One of the men professed a mysterious illness - "nervousness," so he couldn't look for honest work - honest but boring. He had no skills, no training.

But apparently he wasn't so "nervous" he couldn't drive 2,000 miles for a free life style in the Golden State. On arrival he was promptly settled in a two bedroom apartment in beautiful Sunnyvale - the apex of personal brilliance, achievement and technology. The working citizens of California picked up all his bills, including health coverage and his sex change.

As a personal observation, his free sex change was a dismal failure. He was neither fish nor fowl afterward.

Pretty damned clever manipulation, I'd say.

As an aside, have you ever noticed how open, accepting, sharing and forgiving a Liberal is? When there are riots, smashing high-end store windows, smashing windshields of citizens' cars, burning cars and over-turning garbage cans, the Liberal is the first to light a candle, sing, "We shall overcome…" and hug an officer?

But have you ever noticed when a Liberal has his car window smashed, his car tires slashed he is the first to scream "FOUL!" the loudest and the longest! I have found them to be extraordinarily intolerant when it comes to a transgression against their self. Interesting.

(Like Rumpelstiltskin, one of my Liberal friends was so angry when she read this, she smashed her foot through the floor - theoretically.)

22. SOUTH AFRICA

South Africa is a country of 54 million people. 13 million people work and pay taxes, 17 million are on welfare. So, yes, there are more people on welfare than work in South Africa.

In the United States of America the population is 323 million people, 158 million on the work force. Approximately 52 million people are on welfare.

The general economy of South Africa is bleak. That was about as clear a comment as I could find on their government site. In general, current information on subsidies, grants and welfare system in South Africa is garbled, not forthcoming, obscure, verbose - all rhetoric.

This strategy in Communication is called "parsing", telling you the *exact* truth, not in "everyday" communication. Parsing is very clever and misleading. One way you're told the exact truth is by *leaving words out* of information, you assume what is meant. Very clever. Not wrong, just very right.

But the implication is, that in South Africa there are more people on welfare (grants) than pay taxes, so the economy cannot sustain the cost of welfare, or their own government.

Is this the imminent fate of the United States of America?

To read the economics and structure of a country is to learn only facts; such as: The area it encompasses, population, imports-exports, perhaps the breakdown of the population. But you're told nothing about the living conditions of the people - the big WHY they're poor…

So… *WHY* ARE THEY POOR?

If you want to know the truth about any situation, go to a person who lives there, ask them the conditions of the people - go to the horse's mouth.

I have a friend- a citizen of South Africa, who tells me of the actual daily life of the general population. It is not a pretty picture.

South Africa is comparable to America in that the government ostensibly cares about its population. The government has told the people it will create jobs and everyone will be wealthy.

However, South Africa is avidly anti capitalism. Employers are "evil." Capitalists make their money "off the backs of the workers;" the government tells the Capitalists "you are using workers to become rich." To ensure the security of the workers, employers are not allowed to fire anyone for any reason. Get a job and you have that job for the rest of your life whether you work at it or not.

So, here we go, **WHY**…WHY ARE THEY POOR?

EXPENDITURES (South Africa)

Because of government restrictions, employers are reluctant to "hire" employees, so young girls opt for pregnancy for income. For each child they have, girls receive a monthly grant of R300 (about $33.00 American per month). An "R" (Rand) is about $.11 American. Since the allowance for a baby in South Africa is very little, to get more money, they have more babies.

An American welfare payment, in California, is about $638.00 per month for each child. Beside that $638.00, in some areas, there is a rent subsidy, food stamps, health care, and, in some cases there are phone, gasoline and electricity allowances.

And contrary to the information given out by the South African government, my source says the girls there are drinking to excess while pregnant in order to have alcoholic syndrome - sick - babies. That way the girls are assured of a long-term government income. My friend assured me that is absolutely the case.

Income for a sick baby is R1400 per month.

INCOME (South Africa)

Only 13 million people are working out of a population of 54 million people.

The less people they hire, the less taxes are paid.

South Africa is living off its own transfusions, no new blood is coming in to replace the life force of that economy.

If the Liberals have their way, America will be purged of capitalism and everyone will be rich like South Africa.

EDUCATION (South Africa)

A score of 30% is required to pass tests. So, if a student gets 30 questions out of 100, he or she passes the course. If they miss classes, at the end of the term they are to receive the total grade of all their test scores and pass the students on that total. And they are removing math and science from the curriculum because it's too hard to learn.

Kenya

One of my African students gave a speech on the population increase in Kenya. She said the teen age girls there were having babies as fast as they could. She stated that as soon as possible girls would get pregnant and the population had increased there "about 3,000 a day."

She smiled broadly and expected a round of applause from the class. She was met with a dead silence - I was appalled.

I asked, "Who's going to feed all those babies?"

She shrugged her shoulders - indifferent; she looked up at the ceiling - she didn't care.

I'll tell you who will be supporting those children and no doubt thousands more. The good old USA will be tapped to "help the poor little babies." What can poor South Africa (54 million people) do? What can poor Kenya do? They need help. Suddenly it becomes America's problem - give them aid.

Rather, we should send birth control information.

How about Family Planning?

As in America, the welfare is too easy. Countries are poor because they have no interest in lifting themselves up. They know some Do-gooder will rescue them - America! America can't wait to show that we are Benevolent, care about the downtrodden, will help to life up entire nations into the Light - we can't wait to pat ourselves on the back, have some indifferent nation genuflect as an American walks by! We'll rescue you!

And, Kenya, South Africa, will keep their population growth in a fog blaming their situation on anyone but themselves - it works for us.

But, I wonder, when America becomes a third world nation, who will rescue us?

23. EDUCATION IN AMERICA

As an educator, my bias is to educate everyone - *everyone*! to the best of his ability. Much of the time I am criticized for this attitude as people translate education into snobbery, i.e. the more education you have, the *better* you are, *above* others.

Well, that's true, but not in the way some people understand education.

Instead of "education," let's use the word "health." The healthier you are, the better you are. Isn't this reasonable? You *want* to be healthy - it affects the world around you, a positive influence.

Education is mental health. The more achievements, the more wisdom, the more facts, the more understanding, the more control you have over your life, the "better" you are. You understand your worth; you understand the value of the world and the people in it - symbiosis.

With education you can better understand differences, change, social needs, personal needs, the effect of choice, the need for responsibility.

Education is the foundation of healthy growth in social and personal lives.

"I don't judge others!"

I believe the major obstacle to a healthy society, an educated society, is because it takes work, dedication, awareness, a caring for the health - mental and spiritual health, of others - actually, a full-time job!

When someone says, "I don't judge others - it's not for me to say what others should do…," "I don't care what happens to others;

I'm not interested, can't be bothered, not my problem…" they are really saying, "As long as I have what I want, just leave me alone."

This is the height of selfishness!

That's why we're here - to help others, to lift us all up. We cannot have the luxury of ignorance - that is the basis of a sick society. That way, *we all lose*.

EDUCATION IS THE TOOL TO MENTAL HEALTH.

24. PREGNANCY IS A <u>CHOICE</u>

Pregnancy requires no planning, no preparation, no thinking. And from these pathetic conditions we create a new life, a life that has every right to the best of care - a "wanted" child. Every child should have optimum conditions to enter this world; it should not be brought here as the result of someone's libido, or someone's need for ego fulfillment.

Here's an example of flagrant abuse of pregnancy-for-income I've used before:

In Mountain View, CA, on the 6:00 news was a woman with her 15 children and fiancé living in one motel room. She was exhorting the public at large to "help" her - "help" her what? She was intimating that with 15 children there was a need for a constant flow of cash or tangible aid.

A young, well dressed woman nearby stated, "I've done a lot for her, but I can't do any more." I imagine the young woman meant she could not give them any more money - she was tapped out.

Meanwhile, in the background, the mother's "fiance" was resting on the bed with his hands under his head. I assume he was exhausted from incessant breeding.

Had I been there I would have asked him the obvious question, "Why don't you get a job?" Oh, yes, so often people who don't work, but are capable of copious breeding, are "disabled". As Judge Judy says only certain parts of their body work.

We outlaw puppy mills - what about "baby mills?"

Mothers and their fiancees should concentrate on the *quality* of care their children have - *not the quantity* of children they have. The well dressed young woman was aiding and abetting in this charade of pity vs manipulation - she was rewarding bad behavior, a do-gooder.

25. FEMALES <u>DO NOT</u> "GET" PREGNANT

Because a female has a uterus, it is widely assumed she is ordained, obligated, destined to bare children. Why is this mandatory?

We have ten fingers; are we therefore obligated to be a concert pianist? No? Then, why else do we have ten fingers if not to play the piano? You don't need 10 for any other activity.

We have two legs. Therefore we should all run the 10 minute mile. Why not?

A uterus is a vessel, a pot, a bowl which is possible to remain empty. Not all pots are used in your household. Not all bowls are used. We can use one - or not.

A female is an empty vessel until someone fills it. A female does not *"get" pregnant* - she is *impregnat<u>ed.</u> She, in her own right, has no ability to get pregnant.* She needs an outside agent for that condition.

A female's body is a *passive recipient.*

There is one major religion that states if a girl gets pregnant, it's *her mistake.* How can it be *her* "mistake?" I'm so curious to understand what was the mistake she made so we can help other girls avoid it. That "fact" is incredibly stupid.

And, yet, she, alone, is held responsible for her pregnancy. Why? Only in the recent past is a man held accountable for impregnating a female. The male half needs to be implicated in the situation to a serious degree. At present, his "cost" is minimal, and, at times, his participation is minute.

Fines or incarceration don't seem to deter one male from impregnating several females and then flying the coop. Perhaps we need a more serious approach to this indifference to creating a new life. Perhaps we should insist on his participating in the cost of raising a child to a substantial amount.

Jail is not a deterrent. Perhaps the males need to be assigned to an occupation that provides monetary support for the children - support that goes directly to the child. This would show good faith on the part of the father and relieve the taxpayer of some of the financial burden of supporting all his children.

Perhaps this "assigned occupation" could be one that actually teaches a profession, a craft, a skill, an occupation that could reward the father, the child - society…?

On the 6:00 o'clock news a 14 year old girl appeared - for a second time, before a judge in Chicago. She'd been impregnated by her uncle the previous year and, at 13 years old, petitioned for an abortion. The judge refused her petition.

This time, standing before the judge, he sentenced her to prison for being an *unfit mother!*

I was stunned!

Her life was ruined. At 14 years old, she was a mother, an *unfit mother,* and had a criminal record. Where was her life…this *fourteen year old child…*where was *her life? Who cared about her?*

Again, I ask, "Where are all the Right to Lifer's, the Pro Life advocates, the Do-Gooders, the bell-ringing charities, the Liberals who 'shall overcome'… the black veiled stern-faced women who frown on family planning, the placard waving 'All Life is Precious' people - the 'Jesus Loves the Little Children' people - why didn't they help this innocent child in her time of need?"

She was thrown to the wolves.

What happened to the uncle? He was never mentioned again.

One of my male friends was concerned about my implication that men are aggressive and women are innocent, easily used.

He's right. Women can be viable, aggressive manipulators when they have a goal that will benefit them. As a recipient, a woman is not necessarily passive, but even so, she alone, cannot get pregnant.

And, yes, I know girls who got pregnant on purpose thinking the boyfriend would marry them. He didn't. Yes, she made the "mistake," a life changing mistake.

A female under 18 years old, according to the law, is not responsible for her actions. She may, indeed, be very responsible physically, but mentally, and in life experiences, she needs protection, guidance and support. Pregnancy is a serious, life changing condition - a challenge, only for mature, stable women - and men!

26. ADVERTISEMENTS

TV ads, Facebook, dozens of "apps", countless magazines, department store displays, films, to name a few, focus on making their profits off selling "love," youth, beauty, desirability, to girls who have no idea how they're being manipulated.

Girls are shown, coerced, manipulated into provocative poses of how to walk, stand and smile. The ads show copious amounts of flesh awkwardly protruding from "sophisticated" dresses all to attract attention from other women as well as men.

I have seen women, wearing very short dresses, going up escalators, getting up from a chair and bending over to retrieve something near the floor whose dresses were so short their gender was visible and unmistakable. I hung my head in shame for them. They were silently ridiculed and completely unaware of their buffoonery.

Then, they wonder why they get raped, groped, called names and pregnant. Like Carrie Nation, I can't destroy beer kegs but I wish I could put underpants - maybe bloomers - on all the department store dummies and magazine ads that are models for young girls.

Companies rely on advertising to call attention to a new product, a better product or one that's improved, it's called "capitalism." And, it's healthy for the economy.

But, couldn't the concept of quality and good taste be touted as well? Couldn't the concept of decency, modesty, self-respect, be a partner with fashion?

27. FOSTER CHILDREN

On the news tonight they announced that there were so many foster children (in Oregon) that the shelters were full and the state had to place all the extra children in hotels.

When a foster child reaches 18, he or she is shoved out on the street, no Life preparation, no cushion to fall back on, it's heartbreaking. All those beautiful children have no home, no place - no one wants them.

Where are all the "charities" that send out the calendars, the sweatshirts, the tote bags, the address stickers…why haven't they stepped up to the plate to bring these youngsters home to a happy family?

Again and again I ask, "Where are the Right to Life people, all the non-profits - the God-fearing groups? Are not these young lives important?" Every child should have a sanctuary and a feeling of value - it's his and her birthright.

When a child reaches 18, he should have an occupation, something where he can make money, training, an apprenticeship, and above all, a home off the street. The number, 18, is meaningless - it is quality, preparation for self-support, that should be the gauge for independent living.

28. TV PROGRAMS FOCUS ON EMPTY LIVES

There are daily TV programs that focus on the difficulty of being a single mother, the work and stress involved, the lack of support and her dismal future. The role of the father, his responsibility toward the child, his moral support, a show of caring, isn't attended to - never mentioned. Why not?

Recently I watched a program on 20/20 which showed a number of people living in desperate circumstances. They were in some kind of temporary housing. The children, in particular it was said, were affected by the lack of necessities. And yet, some of these children had cellphones and were texting during the program.

What am I missing here?

Maybe we should have classes on priorities to at least upgrade their diet and hold off on the luxuries. One young man (18 years old!) was upset because the school didn't phone him to wake him up so he wouldn't miss classes. His mother worked the night shift and slept in the mornings. So, he stayed home every day - the school dropped him.

If we stop the concept of "disadvantaged," we stop the "benevolent", do-good organizations, then we're losing millions of dollars here, lost wages, lost benefits, lost profits, lost "holier than thou" attitudes, loss of prestige.

"Charity" is **BIG business** - *capitalism*! Do you think that because a business calls itself "non profit" it really is? Are you so innocent that you believe the directors and managers work for free?

Think of all the CEO's out of work! The VP's, COO's, CFO's, assistants, aides, secretaries, grounds keepers - charity is BIG business. The irony is these organizations are viable, but, so many? That are repetitive? All these organizations perform the same functions in a plethora of different forms.

I attended a fund-raising charity function in Carmel by the Sea, CA. It was a concert in a hi-tech tent in the middle of a field. The seats for this concert were extremely expensive; Luciano Pavarotti was featured. After the concert, I asked one of the ushers what the money was for. He replied the Carmel high school needed new polo ponies...new...? *Polo ponies...?*

For once I was speechless. (I can't make this stuff up.)

(It just occurred to me, there are no "disadvantaged" in Carmel.)

What do they do with worn-out polo ponies?

29. CHANGE THE CONCEPT OF "REWARD"

We are paying girls to have children irresponsibly. We are paying them, rewarding them, for bringing children in this world who have no foundation, family, home, or hope for a secure future. This child will live on whatever the "man in the white hat" gives it. The child will have no pride, no dignity, no sense of destiny, only an understanding that it will take whatever it can get, however it can get it and when it can get it - all free.

Do you think that child has not sensed the underlying feeling of "you poor thing"; can you imagine the seeds of rage that are already sprouting?

They are not burdened with the yoke of responsibility, self-discipline, contributing to the strength of a prosperous society. They have no concept of "other" - it's all about what they can get for free - as much and as soon as possible.

Liberals teach the down-trodden to understand that they are entitled to what they get because society at large owes them. At one time there were people who abused others, enslaved them and, so, today these people are entitled to retribution - even-up the stakes. This perception is warped. The past is over. Live TODAY, not in the dead past - contribute energy, your intelligence to helping us all, here and now.

Instead of "rewards" for bad behavior, we need to reverse the perception of reward:

> *Oh, you just had a baby and you don't know who the father is? How unfortunate. Let's take a survey of your companions to find out who'll support you both.*

> *If we cannot locate the father of this child, then it'll be put in*

a foster home or child care where it can get the best care available. Meanwhile, to help you get on your feet, we'll enroll you in school and get you interned in an occupation.

Of course you understand if you don't attend school, or show up at work, your 'reward' will be held in reserve until you complete your internship.

This action should help a disadvantaged person understand the importance of assuming responsibility for his and her *choices*.

30. JUDAISM   ISLAM

Let's pause and look at Judaism and Islam for a moment. Ironically, these two populations have much in common.

They take pride in their children; they look after each other; the young people are closely monitored for optimum living conditions. If there's a problem they close ranks to care for the needs of their people. Their children are carefully monitored so they mature more successfully.

And *there is a father in the home.*

ISLAM: I was touring Egypt with a Muslim, Ahmed, as my guide. My knowledge of Islam is hazy - it seems to be considerably disparate from the general American lifestyle. So, when I need accurate information of some "exotic" lifestyle I always ask a member of that specific population for enlightenment.

I asked Ahmed, "Who runs your government?"

"The Imam (Bishop)." He replied. "The Bishop is a religious leader and also a government leader."

"Who pays taxes?"

"We all do," he replied.

"What about welfare?"

"We have no welfare. We pay our money to the Bishop, to the State. Then we pay our bills. Whatever money we have left over, we put in an envelope and give it to the Bishop (or Mosque) to give to who needs it. We never know who receives it and they never know who gifts it."

This is all done voluntarily to help each other. Muslims do not have a system of "welfare" - it is unthinkable. To have to ask for money is an indication of failure, a cause of shame in their community. They have pride in themselves. Of course from time to time people need financial help, but it's not a way of life.

They don't have thousands of charity "businesses" that are capitalism in sheep's clothing. This way they save millions of dollars that would be spent on CEO's, CFO's, COO's, IT equipment, ergonomic office chairs, individual phones with "app's" for photos, instant dialing, text messaging, and on and on. Capitalism.

Charity, in the American system, strips people of their dignity and an opportunity to grow psychologically and spiritually - it "dumbs" people down. If we don't encourage charities, then we lose business, we lose donations, we lose cushy jobs and fat salaries for the administrators.

JUDAISM: For some years I was a member of a choir in a synagogue. In every service, the Jews uplift themselves in word, music and worship. They are a proud nation; they revere each other, support and help those beyond their religion to uplift the community at large - when they do well, we all do well.

That's a Law of the Universe.

Their children go to school and have productive futures. Their families are a part of the larger community where they help each other. They take great pride in their achievements, in themselves and voluntarily support the community in many ways.

They are often activists, achievers, movers and shakers. They know that if the community at large prospers, so do they. They have only charity in their hearts for the good of all people.

The Jews constitute only .2% of the world's population, but captured 20% of the Nobel Peace Prizes. This is very meaningful in their influence to world peace.

Teaching responsibility by not giving handouts provides people an appreciation of their own value and that of the community. A simple, "Thank you," for taking only what they need allows them to give back as they can.

Thus, nobody owes you anything!

One of the salient characteristics of Jews and Muslims is the strong presence of a male figure in the home. These two groups are concerned about their tradition, their teachings and their image in the community.

For many of us today, the requirements in their traditional lifestyles, seem harsh, unyielding and unfair. But, the family unit is intact, their goals are clear and they do not take from society - they care for their own.

(As an aside, in all the years I did volunteer jail ministering, I only had one Jew in the audience! "Statistically," what does that tell you about Jews as a whole?)

In America, the absence of fathers in the homes is considered to be a determining factor in the cost of welfare and the rise of crime statistics.

We talk a lot about the "fatherless" families in America, and then, do nothing. We shrug our shoulders, "Well, what can we do about it…? It's a shame." End of concern. But there is no end to the welfare payments.

This goes back to the vacuous belief "You have no right to tell people how to live their life." Ok. So why are you *taxing me* to support *them*? What are *my rights*?

31. CHRISTIANITY

Christians loudly profess their stand against abortion - "Right to Life". But, what is the Right to Life organization doing…nothing.

What do the Christians do to stem the flood of welfare babies and all the unexpected, uncared for children? These babies are not planned for, not necessarily wanted and the mother has no training in proper child care. A hit-or-miss childcare system is not acceptable for raising children. There's no father to provide necessities.

What are the Right to Life people doing…*nothing.*

There is the Family Planning organization which many people think is an abortion mill. No - it is **NOT**. It's a place where responsible women and girls can go to plan their babies, take care of their health under the best supervision for optimum health conditions.

A baby has a RIGHT to be born into a warm, loving home where he's wanted and cherished - and, provided for.

Unfortunately, orphanages are full of babies waiting for homes. There are institutions of crack babies sick and abandoned. All these babies-in-waiting are born to mothers who didn't plan for them and don't want them.

If the Right to Life group cared at all for the Right to Life of these unwanted children, there would be no babies abandoned to institutions or the streets. They would all be in loving homes.

I have heard some Christian organizations assure unmarried girls that when they have their baby, "someone" will help them; "someone" will take care of them.

I have asked my young, single female students who had babies, "Who helped you after the birth of your child?" They all said, "No one." - it's all a lie. No one cares about the mother or child, the goal is to stop abortion at all costs.

Abortion is not the answer - responsible family planning is - birth control is responsible family planning.

Can you feel the grief, the hopelessness of not being wanted, unloved, no place to call home, for these innocent lives? What future is there for these babies?

Statistically their destiny may be crime, drugs and homelessness. Then we'll put them in jail for undeserved petty crimes. They were not wanted as children; they're not wanted now.

But, we mean well. I always donate to the Salvation Army bucket at Christmas.

32. WHY UNIVERSAL HEALTH CARE WON'T WORK

I used to think that for a strong society we need two basic elements.

1. Free full health coverage.

2. Free Education.

I thought, "if everyone were healthy and educated we would have the perfect society. Everyone would understand the importance of helping others less fortunate".

Partly true.

Many people insist on comparing health care in Denmark to health care in the USA. In Denmark, health care is free. It's suggested the USA could do the same.

Think about it.

It's like comparing the housekeeping duties between Buckingham Palace and a Swiss chalet.

Absolutely ludicrous.

Realistically universal health care is impractical in the United States. (I truly wish this were otherwise.)

Let's look (rationally) at why.

We could take the gains of the Capitalists - that would pay for all needs of the poor people!

But, wait!!

We've done away with the "filthy" Capitalists - they exploit the poor - remember? There is NO money to provide the necessities of the disadvantaged, because there now are no disadvantaged!! In a socialist country we are all the same! We prosper!

It's a perfect world! Nobody works and we all have everything!

Incidentally, at this writing Denmark is having a financial crisis due to an influx of refugees. The welfare hand-out has substantially increased and Denmark is a small country. The refugees have actually *refused to get jobs*! What can Denmark do in this crisis?

Without Capitalists we have no businesses which equals no jobs. No jobs equals no income, taxes or welfare.

A friend, a young man (early 20's) who comes from a traditional family, 2 brilliant older sisters, mother and father, lovely home. The young man is listless, hates his domineering father. He dropped out of high school but doesn't know what he wants to do.

His mother brings home job applications, helps him fill them out, but he's not interested - he can't "find" himself. Marijuana helps him relax.

Meanwhile, while he's still "looking" for himself, and, while "looking," he managed to sire five children. His mother supported them, but now she has other obligations. He rationally explained he can't find a job that will support all seven of his family, him, his girl friend and their 5 children. The Postal Service was hiring, but it wouldn't support them all on $15.00 hr.(and the marijuana, too).

So, of course, there's welfare! The poor young man, depressed, big family - we must rescue him! Up comes the worker with the White hat on the White horse, "Let me do it for you - you poor thing!"

Myself, I would think with all that libido to produce that many children, he could be put to work splitting logs! It's a way to pass time waiting on his welfare checks.

This is beyond disgusting.

I watch most of the "Judge" shows on TV. I listen to the forensics and usually I'm appalled by the lack of preparation and understanding of the plaintiff or defendant on what is called "evidence" and the complete lack ethics by both parties.

One young woman was being sued; her defense was she was pregnant and couldn't correct whatever the legal problem was. The Judge asked the defendant how old she was, "20 years old." She was also asked, "How many children do you have?" Her reply? "6." SIX! **<u>SIX!!</u>** at 20 YEARS OLD! No schooling. No training in childcare. No marriage - just pregnancies. What does that say about her - about our society?

She hung her head, no eye contact. She was basically a child herself - 20 years old and 6 children. This is the prime of her life; you're only 20 once. She should be in school, developing her intelligence, looking forward to a bright future, enjoying life, not acting as a feather bed for some man's errant libido.

If we have universal health care that means that much of my portion goes to help people like her - a disproportionate amount by far! And, she's only one of hundreds of thousands! The distribution of money is skewed!

In universal health care the money that goes to support one woman's 15 children, another woman's 6 children, another woman's 7 children, and so on, could be better directed for heart transplants, dialysis, insulin, cancer treatments, broken limbs, ulcers, glaucoma - ad infinitum.

And, what about the elderly, infirm people who are dropped off at hospitals like stray animals because they cannot be cared for in their home? These helpless people need professional care, but what do we provide for them? Life-time of contribution to the health of this nation they are "dumped" like stray animals! *So wrong!*

My question is, **WHY**? Why are we paying her, encouraging this woman/child to produce children? She can't pay for her children; she can't provide for them - she has no way to ensure their safety, warmth and future.

If she should ever want to marry, who would want her? Who wants a woman/child who brings with her the burden of sundry children, a mix and match brood of responsibility? When a man looks at her he sees only one thing…and it's *not respect*!

My guess is, she's looking for love and someone to care about *her, for herself!* But, she's looking in all the wrong places - and we're paying her to stay lost.

She's a child herself. We should *insist* she go to school, learn a trade, develop her intelligence, her talents, her self-esteem and an understanding of her value as an individual, so she can take a place in society as a person of quality.

Young people should be in school, planning a strong future, going to parties, doing community work, involved with church, sing in the choir, teach Sunday school, tutor children… enjoy their youth and freedom!

Liberals ask, "Who are you to decide how someone should run her or his life"?

Conversely, I would ask "*Who are you* to encourage people to ruin their lives, stunt their growth and walk in darkness? Keep them oppressed"?

Liberals have little ability to *think* or to *listen*. Their only focus is to *control others* while spouting freedom! And, paradoxically, I believe they really want the best for people! But, their "best" and my "best" are extremely disparate!

Welfare carries the message, "Helpless, dependent, incapable, ignorant, worth-less…let me decide what's best for you, you poor thing."

One young woman in court stated, "He said he had no kid and all his friends had a kid. So I gave him a kid." **GAVE HIM** a kid!

I can't wrap my head around that, *"I gave him a kid."* I understand giving someone a sandwich or a ride home from school, but this is ridiculous!

Not for a moment was any consideration given to the "kid". It was simply a convenience for a relationship, handed over and forgotten. It was the only way the girl knew how to get approval, acceptance and a positive image - love.

It was a testament to the young man - his seed was fertile; it's a rite of passage. Now he's got a kid. He's a real man! As far as they're concerned, the issue is closed, forgotten.

No, not forgotten. You and I will be paying for that child's care for the next 18 years - or more. And, again, that's only one of her "kids."

Another girl with seven children said she planned to look for work a soon as "she got on her feet." I wanted to note, "Well, you can't get 'on your feet' until you get off your back."

Again, someone will say, "You have no right to tell people what children they can have. People have a right to have any children they want."

Yes, I agree - I have no right. *Then let them PAY for their children!* Don't tax me to pay for their pleasures. That's the part people don't understand - someone has many unplanned children and you and I are expected to pay for them! Why?

In my classes I often talk about "rights." My "rights" end where yours begin. Your "rights" end where mine begin.

Stop "illegitimate" birthing - no husband, no pay. Put the kids in foster care. Put the young mothers in school or in jobs - no excuses.

Can you imagine the low self-esteem of these young girls? They have to grovel to young men to accept them. Sex is their way to get companionship, approval and value. Sex, then, becomes cheap and available.

One TV program is devoted to trying to find out who is the father of a girl's baby often from among 1, 2, 3 candidates for that position. The girl is always positive that one of them is the cherished father. Sometimes she's right, and sometimes she's wrong; like roulette, spin the wheel and see which overnighter is the daddy.

Meanwhile this program goes out to millions of viewers. The message is: Don't worry about responsibility. If you get pregnant, someone will take care of you, pay your bills. It's ok to look for a "daddy" in front of millions of viewers.

Every child born deserves a father and a mother, a family unit. No child should be playing roulette, spinning random numbers, hoping the needle stops on "that one's my daddy."

Is this the message we want sent out to our youth? Is this how America wants the "average" TV viewer to model her life? Is this why there are so many delinquents, because from the start they have no father and, essentially, no "mother?"

Who cares about the children? No one. It's all a sham, a hollow game.

I had a student who had a mother and father and they lived together in a house in San Jose. When he was five (5!) years old, his parents split up - the mother went one way and the father went the other. They left the boy at the house. - quite literally, left him - alone!

He went over to the neighbor's who let him live on their porch for the next ten years. The "boy" is now a man of 20 and my heart aches for his pain over all those years where he knew he wasn't wanted.

Where are all the Right to Life people? Where are all the Do Gooders? How can a baby of 5 be left behind by his parents? What kind of people just walk away from *their* child?

Now he has a child and a girl-friend. I pray he doesn't follow in his father and mother's footsteps.

Universal health care would cost far more than the tax payers can provide. There are hundreds of thousands of ill people who need on-going, intensive care but the tax funds are siphoned off by selfish individuals who have no interest in anyone but themselves. This way of life should be discouraged.

When America distributes the funds for "well-fare" correctly, we can easily have the health care we need, free, for *everyone*.

33. PROVIDE BIRTH CONTROL

If we really do care about an unborn child, if we really *cared for the child* so it's loved and provided for, then, as we say in America, "Put your money where your mouth is." We need emphasis on education to avoid pregnancy until people can provide for a child. Children need a solid home and care; *it's their right.*

Teach young people - unmarried people in particular, boys and girls, the importance of having a place for a child, before pregnancy. There should be considerable preparation, beforehand-thinking, *intelligent, thoughtful* planning, "Can we afford this"? Where will the money come from to pay all the expenses?

Family planning

Much of the idea of welfare is to help women who are pregnant or who have children with no father, income or home. Contrary to that belief, *women do not need help with pregnancy - it is no problem to get pregnant! The solution is, to help them - teach them how to **stop** getting pregnant.*

And this teaching must start early, start in the lower grades, not when they're in puberty and under the control of hormones.

34. SAVE WELFARE PEOPLE FROM EXPECTATION OF FAILURE.

One student, a young man, asked to meet me privately to discuss a problem he was having. It seems he had an opportunity to go into business with someone and this was a goal his heart was hoping for - success, financial independence and high self esteem.

The problem was his "homies", his buddies. He was part of a close knit group of young men. They were united against his "changing" who he was - or, who he thought he should be.

If he had a business, he couldn't hang out with them - he'd be working. He'd set himself apart. If he "changed", by definition, then they "changed". If he becomes successful, then, by comparison, they are losers, failures. To them, this is intolerable. But, to achieve and grow must seem either insurmountable to them, or frightening. They're weak, fearful of the unknown, fearful of change.

He asked me what he should do. If he went into business, he'd lose his "family". If he didn't go into business, he'd be locked into a dead-end life; this was his chance to succeed, make something of himself.

I said, "You have no 'decision' - you have to go into business. If those men were your 'friends' they would cheer you on, support you in anything you wanted to do. They want to hold you back; hold you down. You can't allow that. If they cut you out, you'll have to find new friends."

He sat there, very quiet, in the empty classroom. I left.

In another class I had a most unusual configuration, I had 4 males and 4 females of a specific ethnicity. In the male group I had one student who was exceedingly intelligent, self-determined and self-possessed as well as handsome.

He spoke French fluently, wrote poetry and eventually became the school Valedictorian.

When he gave presentations in class his 3 buddies would throw spitballs at him, paper airplanes, guffaw, shuffle their feet and in any way, do what they could to throw him off-balance.

Their tactics never worked. Not for one instant did the other 3 confuse or fluster him. He never got upset or betrayed the slightest inconvenience.

Needless to say, I was very upset. Under no circumstances do I allow students to annoy or bother anyone for any reason. I told them to stop their bad behavior - which they did.

But, his "friends" tried their best to keep the Valedictorian "down" at their level of ignorance, their level of low self-esteem. If he became educated, moved ahead in life, he would be different from them - they'd lose him, and, in a sense, themselves.

Of the other 4 in the same ethnicity, 3 of the girls had no eye contact with me at any time; they were totally disinterested in school - except for one girl - let's call her Sue. She was exceptionally bright, completely caught up in the class content.

When I lectured, she hung on every word. Her eyes snapped at every comment I made. Sue was hungry, starved for information, education.

Sue had talked to another instructor about a problem in her life. It seems she loved school and was doing well, but her 3 friends were angry with her. They told her, "Stop being so smart" or they wouldn't speak to her again.

She didn't want to lose her friends but she wanted to stay in school. She sat there, sobbing; what to do? The instructor told her the same as I would, "These are not your 'friends' - move on."

But only people with families who understand the value education, self-esteem, know-how, have the ability to "move on;" it hasn't subtlety been drummed into them that "they can't succeed".

My five year old granddaughter had trapped herself on a net ladder in the sandbox at the park. Her feet were somewhat tangled in the rope squares so she couldn't get loose to move. As she hung on with her hands, she looked over at me with a pitiful expression on her face, "Help me, untangle me;" her eyes begged me to set her free.

Nope. My eyes told her, "You got in that mess; you get yourself out." And, she did. She figured it out and took charge of her life. It would have been so easy for me to step into the sandbox and untangle her, but she would have been cheated of a successful experience, cheated of knowing she had charge of her life, control of her destiny.

Today she's in college training for her R.N. In a responsible job like that there are times you have only yourself to make critical decisions; there's no one there to bail you out. You need to know you can trust yourself. What a great feeling!

The point is the Well-meaning Haves, the Do-gooders have drummed a mantra into a huge chunk of the population:

You're disadvantaged; you're going nowhere - you can't do it; you'll fail. Listen to ME! Let ME keep you down, keep you labeled, discouraged. You're a failure without ME!

35. TWO-SIDED VIEW

Imagine welfare as a two-sided view. The Do-gooders look at the Have-nots and feel sorry for them as though they were specimens in a petri dish.

Benevolent Ones: "Oh the poor things. They can't help themselves; they live in bad neighborhoods, so many children. No hope in their future; just a dismal life."

The Have-nots stare back, amused, at the Do-gooders, thinking,

"Feel sorry for us all you want, you... (insert racist name of your choice. The downtrodden have no censorship on what names to call main stream people - we have to understand them). Just keep the checks comin' in!"

Can you imagine how the Do-gooders are being duped? They just keep sending out checks and donations and feel uplifted about their charity work.

Who's winning here?

Now, having said all this. Let's look closer. Who controls the monies for taxes; who decides what amounts go where? Who says who is qualified for assistance and how much? What group or individual controls the incoming money for distribution to the needy?

How much does it cost the taxpayer to distribute the funds? How many departments are there to distribute funds? How many people handle the funds? How many government employees are directly connected to the collection, maintenance and distribution of this specific allocation of taxes? Are they interested in changing the system?

What do you think?

36. CESAR CHAVEZ: "A Man Must Have Dignity"

My goal for this book is to bring into sharp focus the disparity between the Haves and the Have-nots. The Haves enjoy self esteem, self-pride, an understanding of their value, their contribution to uplift the society around them and their ability to guide those to the "light".

There are many good people in this world who give of themselves to others, and unselfishly lift everyone up. These people dedicate their life to help people who have little education, understanding of their value and direction of how to make basic changes to move forward.

As a Mexican American raised in the despair of the Great Depression Cesar Chavez understood the various levels of poverty: Despair, hunger, hopelessness, embarrassment, shame. He understood the toll these feelings had on a family, a people who had centuries of pride in their history.

In the Great Depression the Chavez family lost their home due to back taxes. After decades of back-breaking work as ranchers in Arizona - the family heritage - gone. They were poor - homeless.

They migrated to California where Cesar felt the first sting of prejudice. The "obreros" the "campesinos", farm workers were paid very little and cheated of some of their pay; they worked long hours and were bullied and ridiculed by the foremen at the farms. Chavez was outraged.

Every night after work he'd visit, 1, 2 workers, at their homes, patiently explaining the need to organize, stand up for each other, the Mexicans, Chinese and Filipinos - all the farm workers.

With the help of the Catholic priests and the energy of the farm workers, he got the obreros' wages increased and established the United Farm Workers Union. A truly amazing task of his energy and devotion to lifting up his people.

All through his speeches, meetings with people - *all people*, he said, over and over,

"A man must have dignity."

Dignity does not come from welfare. Dignity comes from understanding the value of one's self. Dignity does not come from the outside, it comes from the inside, an understanding of self-worth through education and enlightenment.

Along with dignity, Chavez was an *advocate of **non-violence***. Never, *never*, in any of his demonstrations, his group meetings or his appearances, did he allow one moment of violence. Demonstrators did not smash store windows, car windshields, assault police or firemen, throw stones, commit arson or hurt people. It was unthinkable! He was an ethical, a man of peace and genuine caring for others.

As a man of dignity and intelligence; he brought out those traits in others, violence is a betrayal to one's self. Violence tells that you cannot win by self-respect, you can only win by destruction. But, you will end up destroying yourself; "If you live by the sword, you die by the sword."

A man must have dignity.

Education is paramount to strengthen and understand self-worth. For a "man to have dignity" - his place in the world, he has to meet the social standard of accomplishments and the basics of economic survival which is grounded in education.

I was fortunate to meet his son-in-law, Richard Ybarra when he spoke at Foothill College. It was inspiring. He is a man who carries on the tradition of peace, helping others, building others up, education and pride in his heritage.

A man must have dignity.

At this point in time the Catholic Church is considering canonizing Chavez. He is a Saint; he's far above others in his devotion to uplift us all by peaceful means. He is an excellent example of the right way of life.

We have much to learn from Cesar Chavez.

37. AFTER THE FACT

At this present time, all the consulting, guidance and modeling that we have done for people in need is done *after the fact*. We Haves assume people in general understand the Rules of Society the same way we do.

They don't.

We Haves make some aggressively erroneous assumptions that all society will understand our message and know we are disseminating Truth, "Let the Man help you; we'll do it for you because you can't do it for yourself." An absolute insult.

Some levels of Rules are too lax, too arbitrary, for mainstream America to understand - we are deluded.

Rules need tightening up for everyone's sake.

Everyone needs self-respect and approval from others. And to get respect from society at large, we have to follow the rules of that society - in this case, Mainstream America.

Mainstream America should model respect for self and others. We should teach respect - for everyone, starting in the first grade and reinforced throughout the school life. Anticipate problems, nip them in the bud.

Any hint at bullying should be immediately addressed and the energy re-directed.

Don't wait until some teen gets pregnant and then needs aid; don't wait until some young man gets picked up for selling drugs or robbing a 7-11. Anticipate problems, have better choices of life styles for young people. Teach them to appreciate all this wonderful country has to offer.

We need to provide on-the-job training, home-making, budgeting, nutrition classes for *everyone* in school. Have a male cook as a model for boys; men make terrific cooks! Girls can repair cars.

School should be mandatory. When I was a kid I had to attend school! There was no alternative - we cared about the children. We cared about their well-being.

We had truant officers - we were tracked! What happened? When did we stop caring? Ask a Liberal.

SOLUTIONS TO UPDATE WELFARE

It's easy to say, "That 'otta' be fixed..." when an idea or commodity isn't functioning well. To suggest ideas to fix this problem we need another level of creativity. We made it abundantly clear, if not always acceptable, or reasonable, that welfare needs to stop, change, update, or, at least, **serious**, review. It's a burrow, a labyrinth of monetary waste and a travesty of human dignity.

Any help or assistance to the public should be what will *help* them through a bad patch, not increase their dependence on aid.

Why are we fostering weakness, helplessness, losers, in a country founded on independence, freedom, creativity and self-direction?

Give people the pleasure, the pride, the uplifting feeling of accomplishment, a feeling of winning on their own merit. Teach them skills, teach self-respect. Praise them for a job-well-done. Provide birth control, self-discipline, raise self-esteem - ethics...*dignity*!

A human cannot live without dignity. We need to understand our self as having value. We were created out of Love - we cannot survive without *dignity*.

- STOP THE MONEY - START SELF-RESPECT

The American Middle Class cannot continue to support a population of "takers", people who syphon the wages of the middle class workers; takers have no respect for the monetary sacrifice of worker families. The "takers" are rapidly outnumbering the "supporters". The American Middle Class is being ripped off - financial suicide, social suicide.

We, ourselves, are killing the goose that lays our golden eggs.

ISN'T THIS OBVIOUS?

But, if we, the middle class complain, and don't see the Emperor's new clothes, we're labeled: Racist, homophobic, selfish, Capitalists, reactionaries and many more vacuous epithets.

As an experiment, I asked one class to define or explain the words: Racism, race, homophobic, capitalist, bigot, reactionary and Hispanic.

Not one *(!!) student,* **college** *student (!) could define any of the above epithets; yet the words are freely bandied about in demonstrations of bigotry. This situation is a prime example of ignorance - inexcusable! Unacceptable!*

The middle class need to change labels to: Intelligent, sensible, cautious, thrifty, appreciated, leaders in-charge and wise. We must stop being used as deep pockets so charities and others feed their ego at our expense.

As American citizens, we cannot allow this perception of degeneration to continue. We must stop suffocating people "in need", stop poisoning their minds by describing them as "poor", "helpless", "unable to work," "unteachable, slow" and the ultimate insult, "disadvantaged."

It's **NOT TRUE!.**

As Barnum of Barnum and Bailey said, "People will believe the person who talks the loudest and the longest." We must change the mantra!

This lack of pride in one's self is a breeding ground of crime and wanton destruction. People who are successful in society's norm don't destroy property; they don't litter their lives with graffiti and garbage. But, if you tell people they're no good, they will do no good. This is not how we want the population of our nation to live and perceive themselves.

We are feeding people on a diet of social poison - welfare. We need to change their diet to the substantive concepts of success, lift themselves up with inner pride of who they really are - capable, intelligent, individuals.

Following are steps to guide people to a satisfactory life style of self-respect and self-esteem:

- *LISTEN* TO GIRLS, TAKE THEM SERIOUSLY

This is first on my list because it's rare, and, so necessary.

It's unusual for someone to listen to a girl, to take her seriously.

Over all the years when I have been confused, hurt and in mental anguish from life's vicissitudes, I sought help from counselors, pastors, priests, friends and strangers; the responses I got were:

you don't really mean that

you don't really feel that way

well, what did you do to cause this?

well, (he, she, it) has their side, too.

you should get over it

just move on

give it time

you need a man

you just have to accept them like that

that's the way they are

Silence and a blank look are often the main response.

Girls seek love, approval and rational guidance. Even with the advent of Women's Lib, it has not taken hold strong enough to persuade society in general to perceive girls as persons to be respected in their own right.

The #metoo movement is a start - it's 70 years late, but a start.

Tradition and family perception of girls still holds fast to the dark ages where girls were to be a helpmeet to men. When a young man seems to appreciate the girl's charms, says the words she longs to hear, seems to listen to her and support her dreams, she assumes the young man loves her - he doesn't - and she gets pregnant. It's not love that motivates him to gaze into her eyes - it's hormones.

Girls need someone to talk honestly and openly to them - someone who *cares* about *them.* Tell the girls the unvarnished, cold reality of Life. No platitudes, no what "should" be; tell them *what is* and how to fix it.

Girls don't understand how they're being used, demeaned, insulted; they see pregnancy as acceptance, having value and having someone to love. I've heard interviews where single pregnant girls say, "I wanted something to love."

How sad. Perhaps they were not born into a loving family and there was no one to give them the sweet attention every child deserves.

Talk to them, woman to woman. Tell them about the rewards of a career, finding a path of life that will help them be a person satisfied with themselves and they can be proud of what they, themselves, have done under their own ability. Show them they can be proud of what they have learned, studied, mastered and how the world has opened up for them.

Bring in women who are attorneys, doctors, accountants, pilots and more to talk to girls about how great life and achievements are. Explain to the girls that children are a gift that should have the advantages of a home, a family and stability. Those advantages can come when the girl is mature and can understand the responsibility of a family.

When a young, single girl has children, her life is over - that child is her life. She has a commitment for the next 18 years, if not longer. She will miss out on dances, fun at the beach, hanging out with friends - all her youth - *gone.* This is not fair to her. She needs to know how precious youth is, how blessed she is to have fun and friends and a future.

Young men also need to know they have value other than for making babies. They seem to need to prove their virility, their manhood. Instead they should be lauded for their incredible intelligence, their artistry and their inner and outer strength.

They are beautiful people in their own right.

- LOVE

It's all around you in songs. Turn on any radio, TV, phone, humming, random singing, group fun - the lyrics will, very probably, be about "love". It seems all the world needs now is "love."

Not exactly.

What about "truth", common sense, self esteem, respect for self and others…? Can anyone define "love"?

> *One woman I know was married 3 times. Each marriage ended in an ugly divorce. Yet she maintained each of her marriages was "true" love. She never woke up. She's still looking for True Love #4.*

> *One woman I know was married 3 times. Each marriage ended in an ugly divorce. Yet she maintained each of her marriages was "true" love.*

> *She never woke up. She's still looking for True Love #4.*

"True love" comes when you are physically mature, supporting yourself, thinking clearly about the attributes and failures and success of yourself and your partner. No one is perfect and no one is lost. A good marriage, like a good partnership, takes sharing and respect for each other. Accept the snoring, the bald head, the grey hairs… respect the person that puts up with your faults. That's love.

- SEX

No, it's not love - necessarily. At times sex is a substitute for companionship, appreciation, acceptance, warmth, caring - and fun. But, it's not love. Girls need to clearly understand love and sex are two separate events. Real love is wonderful, sex may get you pregnant - and alone, on welfare, dead end.

- RESPECT

Respect must go in both directions. The "poor," the "unfortunate," *and* the Middle Class all deserve respect. All too often the middle class is treated like the bad guy, the rich guy, holding up wealth from others who want it without working for it. And the middle class then feels apologetic for perceived success as though they inherited success from their grandfather - a "freebee."

And, in reality, the middle class looks down on less successful people; they would never admit to that, or course, it's just not done. But in their heart they don't want to associate with losers.

Disrespect must not be tolerated in any direction. To "understand" someone by allowing disrespect cannot be tolerated.

- FAMILY PLANNING

This is an intelligent approach to having happy, healthy and wanted children. There is no greater gift to a child than to be prepared for, hoped for and wanted.

There are well-qualified agencies as well as doctors who can advise the best times for pregnancies and how many children that mother should have - or not.

It's *quality* that matters in a family - not quantity.

- BIRTH CONTROL

Some major religions do not allow birth control. Why not? Apparently the assumption is that women are not responsible enough to space their children or make a conscious decision when to get or not get, pregnant.

In these religions a woman's choices or needs are controlled by a preacher, a priest or some self-appointed messiah.

This is the epitome of arrogance.

Girls on welfare who are impregnated by "accident", carelessness or design should be encouraged to work, go to school, or both. While the girls are in school getting *satisfactory* grades, they can have financial assistance and the babies will be in day care, foster homes or child care.

There's no husbandless pregnancies, no recreational pregnancies, until individuals can pay for their children themselves - no tax payer support. But if people choose to get pregnant for income, then put the children in foster care so the parent can go to school or work.

Being a parent is a huge responsibility not to be taken lightly. But once done, they are responsible - not society.

Unfortunately, it's not uncommon for a father to disengage from responsibility of family care. It's a lot of trouble to pay for rent, food, clothes, medical aid, etc. for his children. For a healthy family unit father and mother are both necessary; a child needs assurance from both people for a strong self-image.

- EDUCATION SCHOOL: MANDATORY

Education is a key to success. Education is a foundation for self-esteem, self-pride. Perhaps school is not the whole answer, but it certainly is a huge chunk of it - if only for self-esteem.

> *I think about when my husband walked out on me and my two girls. My self esteem was crushed. I had no job skills, no education. How was I to survive with my children? For awhile I was a part-time waitress, a house cleaner and part time switch board operator. I managed to pay the rent and eat, but this was not a way to survive. I needed some serious job skills.*

> *I enrolled in a community college in "easy" courses because I was terrified I'd fail. My self esteem was shredded. I moved along slowly, step by step until I found something I could do well.*

> *I passed the easy courses and little by little I gained confidence. It took 6 years, but by the time I graduated with an M.A. I had pride and faith in my self. School helped lift me up.*

Learning is up to the individual - you can't force anyone to learn. But we can provide incentive. We need class content tailored to the community. Not everyone will be a poet or expound philosophy. We need plumbers, car mechanics, teachers, nurses, cooks, etc.

School should be practical; emphasize mathematics, reading comprehension, understanding contracts, communication skills, relationships - things we use everyday - subjects that are easily recognized as being in our daily lives.

Provide on-the-job training, home-making, budgeting, nutrition classes for *everyone* in school. Have a male cook as a model for boys; men make terrific cooks! Girls can repair cars

School should be mandatory. When I was a kid I **had** to attend school! There was no alternative - we cared about the children; their "well fare" - faring well, doing well. What happened?

School should also be mandatory in jails, prisons, foster care, homes. You're never to old or too young to learn something new and useful. Have goals: Apprentice, Journeyman, Master, guidelines to show progress, skills.

- PUT EVERYONE AGES 18 TO 55 TO WORK

Give everyone the opportunity to feel useful, wanted, capable and creative.

Provide internships, pay them wages, If they don't make it to work, there's no "pay," no "help" because I'm disadvantaged - well, yes, tutoring.

Put **everyone** to work; clean graffiti, clean gutters, paint walls, fix windows, rake leaves, work at the animal shelters, people shelters, old folks homes, clean the beaches, repair windows, tear down abandoned houses, clean the streets, pull weeds in vacant lots - I see something to do where ever I go (I'm OC).

And, the Salvation Army always needs volunteers, workers, and they will train you so you can have some skills in the world of technology and people skills.

Give the "disabled" work to do commensurate with their abilities - everybody can do *something*! Among other changes, we will strengthen self-esteem.

Lift people up; instill genuine pride.

I have a disabled daughter who has limited movement and is in a wheelchair. Sometimes she drops something and it's a struggle for her to pick it up.

She tries and tries. Moves her wheelchair back and forth, stretches out her hand and uses the tips of her fingers to reach it. She is determined to get the object on her own.

It's painful for me to watch her struggle; I could, so easily pick up whatever she wants and hand it to her. But if I do that the covert message tells her that she's incompetent, a failure - useless.

I let her struggle and when she does manage to grasp the object, she has a feeling of elation, achievement. Everyone deserves that opportunity to "win" on their own.

Everyone can do something; we need a feeling of accomplishment, self pride.

Nobody gets a free ride - why should they? Everyone should contribute to the success of their society, their life, in any way they can.

Where will the money come from for all this? The money we don't pay out for irresponsible breeding!

Pregnancy is not an "accident"; we can insist on "accident" insurance. There are many choices of birth control, freely distributed.

- STOP DIVISIVE LABLES

Discard the "us-them" labels. We are not Hispanics, Native Americans or African Americans - we are AMERICANS; this is the _UNITED_ STATES of AMERICA.

If the situation requires labels, let them be: Americans, citizens, Texans, the people on the west coast, California girls…, let the labels be accurate and inclusive.

- STOP DERISIVE LABLES STOP THE GREEK CHORUS:

"You're disadvantaged"

As long as we hammer that label into their minds **"you're disadvantaged,"** people will believe it. After all, you and I are the experts! We have stamped their foreheads with the word "LOSER" - they're branded.

Change the mantra: You're intelligent! You're bound for success! That was a good decision! You're independent; self-determined - figure it out!

At one college where I taught Communication Studies the school made it a point to include disadvantaged people in our classes. As it turned out, that was a poor idea.

The students who came to class were not prepared for college. They had no understanding of time schedules, study techniques, had limited vocabulary and no idea of reading textbooks. Often they just dropped out.

Also, often I had a very hard time understanding their "patois". It was embarrassing.

Much of my teaching experience was also a learning experience for me. Even among Americans I entered new worlds of communication styles that were alien to me. But, I did appreciate the opportunity to open up my understanding of other cultures.

*Another student, same college, was a young boy - I say boy"
because he was very slender, smooth face, tall and gangly.
Very likable.*

*He was recruited from Arkansas for the football team. He
had a campus guide who went to most of his classes and, in
general, introduced him to our school.*

*He missed a lot of my classes and his excuse for not doing
class work was, he said, he had no textbook. I gave him
mine. He was not doing well and did not participate in the
class discussions.*

I suspect he didn't understand our California accent.

*I was told by his guide that if I didn't pass him, he'd be sent
home to Arkansas. However, that is not the basis on which
students pass my class. I had offered to tutor him in **any** of
his classes. He was very pleased but I never saw him again.*

This was another case of well-meaning Do-gooders. I wonder if
we just reinforced this young man's belief of being inadequate,
stupid?

To me, this covert message is inexcusable as well as personally
painful. We are cheating him out of a wonderful, self-discovery,
self-growth experience.

I did try to explain to the school this was not a good idea, but
there was no verbal response only a disgusted glare at me, the
message being "You don't understand - you don't care about the
'disadvantaged'."

And, of course, I am wondering how academics can be so stupid.
A PhD does not ensure intelligence.

- TUTORING

On four occasions, at colleges, requests were made to help (tutor) the students who were having difficulty passing the courses. Of course, in all four cases, I volunteered to help. I enjoy tutoring.

In one ethnic group I was told I was not wanted as I was not one of them. Again, for a similar group, my application was ignored. Another group (a large group) was holding classes in the auditorium. At that group, I was *physically shoved, backward out the door,* being told, "You're not one of us."

I was stunned! What does this say about those groups sincerely wanting help? What incentive do they have to change?

Ignorance is the tail wagging the dog.

- JOB TRAINING <u>EVERYONE</u> WORKS

Internships, on-the-job training, is a good way to teach job skills. Everyone at a job-skill class is "equal", no one excels in job training. If they're above average, get them a job and move them out!

On-the-job training is fun, practical and useful. Basic skills are greatly needed in the work force. So many times I hear a foreman say, "I can't get help!" in the blue-collar jobs. Those jobs have great unions, good hourly wages and job protection - a good way to get a foundation in work ethics.

- DAY CARE

Provide day care for low-income mothers while they're in school or at work. Or put their children in foster care. Mothers should have time to study and have child-care help so they can attend school and benefit from the opportunities education provides.

- FOSTER HOMES

When girls have children their care interferes with the individual progress of the mother. She can't go to school and study or work an 8 hour shift if she has duties at home with the children.

They can be placed in foster homes; the mother can have them weekends or after school visits.

- **COUNSELING** Build up their self-esteem, self-pride

Discuss *why* people choose to be on welfare when jobs are plentiful, education is available, tutoring, help of many types is available, child care, transportation, and more, are offered as help.

Why do people want to be demeaned, looked down on, feel hopeless and unsuccessful when everything they need is ready and waiting for them to take charge of their life, to experience independence - financial independence.

Many people don't understand their value and their talents. Counseling could show them a better life than welfare. They could be uplifted and help bring this wonderful country to a place where everyone is developing his and her optimal talents. It's a win-win.

38. ALL YOU WANT IS MONEY!

Have you ever loaned a friend some money? You couldn't spare it, you needed it yourself - but, this was a friend and he needed it so you loaned it to him. As time passed he made no effort to return it, but bought a 'cycle, took his girl friend to 'Vegas and had a big BBQ.

Concerned about the money he's throwing away, you mention payment for the loan. Suddenly, you're the bad guy! Your "friend" un-friends you; it seems all you want is money! He needed your help and now you want the money back - how could you do this to him! You're selfish! He thought you were a friend!

He turns on you and you're surprised!

Welfare recipients don't "thank" someone for the help - they just want more. Once you hand over a dollar to someone, suddenly it's *theirs* - there's no concern about how it got there or the responsibility of returning it.

When you request the return of a "loan" or stop giving money, then hate, destruction and name-calling result.

39. PEOPLE LEAVING AMERICA

One of my neighbors just left for Costa Rica. Other friends are leaving for Canada and England. They're preparing for the social explosion in our society - the dissolution of America. The explosion is inevitable - the Haves vs the Have-nots; but I'm not sure if any serious changes at this point would be entertained by our society, no matter how rational.

If there is a social explosion it will come from the division of the rich vs the poor with the working class caught in the middle. The middle class is suffering, trying to balance the skewed load of outgo vs reduced income.

The middle class essentially supports the nation, pays all the bills for the Haves and the Have-nots. The government takes care of itself while welfare explodes with the hand-out population. When the middle class goes down, America shuts down - we all lose.

I had one friend discuss this with me. She is looking forward to when the day comes (the "After the Revolution Day" to quote her, meaning the day the Have-nots will take over leadership of America) she'll have everything she wants. I asked "If America shuts down, who will send out the welfare checks?" She didn't respond - she's on welfare, not her problem - *it's your problem.*

It seems that there are politicians, also, who feel there is an imbalance of wealth and that we should be take from the rich and give to the poor. I find that amusing - they're all millionaires! RICH!! They're looking for votes - it's what the majority want to hear. They don't give a damn about the tax payer - and, they ain't about to give up any of their capital!

I suddenly had a flashback to when I was even years old. We were just pulling out of the Great Depression and many people were getting welfare - "relief", thanks to F.D. Roosevelt. The money and help at that time were genuinely needed, but I, in my seven year old mind, was told they were all freeloaders by people fortunate enough to have jobs.

Apparently I was a nuisance one day so my mother sent me off to write a poem about relief:

People on relief just lay in bed

Where people who work have to earn their bread.

The fat politicians by the workers are fed

they have no cares or worries

while the taxpayers live in dread.

Yes, the scan is off - so whatd'y' want from a 7 year old? But the idea of "free" money sure caught on. Apparently I was taught early on the concept of self-determination and pride.

Don't the politicians understand that if America goes down, so do they?! As it is today "rich" people live in homes surrounded by guards, dogs and surveillance systems. Is that "living?" How long will the guards and the dogs last in a plundering mob? At that point money will have no meaning; it will be a matter of survival, whatever it takes.

The old example, "It's like shoveling sand against the tide;" the middle class cannot shovel fast enough to stem the tide of the increasing welfare cost.

40. THE HOMELESS

I was asked if I would mention the homeless in this book. This is an entirely different population: Some are drug addicts who have dropped out of reality; some are free spirits who cannot be boxed in. Some are desperados, on the lam from paying child support or a bank robbery 10 years ago and some are hiding out from a dangerous husband or boy friend.

And, others have hit a bad patch in life; these people need help and are trying to help themselves. There are agencies to help these people relocate, find jobs and lift themselves up to better circumstances. This type of aid makes good sense.

Again, this is the opportunity for the churches, synagogues, mosques, wards and temples to put their money where their mouth is. Step up to the plate! Put up shelters in the vast recesses of your classrooms, storage rooms, auditoriums, study halls, theaters - put your free, self-aggrandizing income to good use.

The best we can do for the homeless is offer a place to stay, briefly, for shelter, a bath (hopefully), medical care and food. Their goal of the homeless is not to breed for income, but to be left alone 'til they can move on.

If you would like to buy a homeless person a meal, a night's lodging, but, like me, don't want to give them money for drugs, you could make an arrangement with a local diner or motel.

Perhaps you could buy a supply of "tickets" from businesses who understand your motivation; i.e., gift tickets for: one breakfast, one hamburger lunch, one night in a motel with hot showers and a warm bed. These would be non-refundable gifts to the recipient, to be used only as designated.

This way, you could feel good knowing you're doing the right thing; if the person is really in need, you've helped him. And those homeless persons or those who sincerely want help, will know there are people who care, who understands them and cares about them. This is a win-win.

When I was touring Scotland, I checked out a public "shower house" (my name, not theirs). For a very small amount you get clean towels, privacy and a great, hot shower! I didn't need a shower, but loved the idea!

WHERE THE MONEY WILL COME FROM FOR THE PROGRAMS

Step 1. To start, stop payments for additional children born to single girls. Take the children she has in the home and put them in day care or foster homes. Put the mother to work so she can pay her own way. If she's in school, we pay for her child care and living costs until she graduates.

Like *all working mothers*, she has to have care for her children while she works. So, of course child care is provided by the tax payers.

If she has additional children while in school or at work, put the child in foster care. It is NOT better for a child to stay with it's mother when the mother is irresponsible, single and cannot afford it.

Girls need to understand their life will improve without the responsibility of child rearing when they're single. The time to have children is after marriage, in a home and a steady income. Then you have the blessing of having children that are wanted, loved and happy in society.

It is understood that if the mother is on drugs, she will lose the children until she's clean.

Step 2. When we stop irresponsible breeding, and have only children we want and can afford, the crime rate will drop exponentially as well as the cost of the prison facilities, cost of the inmates, the lawyers, paperwork, sundry employees.

Step 3. Provide dormitory housing for all single welfare recipients. The cost to maintain separate living quarters for all needy people is extremely impractical. If people are not happy in dormitory quarters, they can provide their own housing.

Such as the two men who drove to California from Arkansas for an increase in welfare payments. They got all they asked for, and more. Outrageous!

Step 4. Stop the rampant, tongue in-cheek, not-for-profit capitalists. Require all charities to pay their total cost of the government and infrastructure - especially property taxes. This, alone, will, *substantially*, increase our ability to "save souls" in this world!

FINALE

And, yes, there are people who say, "It's not that easy." Who said anything about easy? Is it "easy" now? We Americans must slow the increase of population based on hand-outs, increase in crime and irresponsible reproduction. Without some kind of responsible monitoring, our destiny to social suicide is inevitable. Is this what we want?

The above proposed changes in society are based on common sense and the good life for ***all*** Americans.

It's the right thing to do.

THE FISHERMAN AND HIS WIFE

Brothers Grimm

Once upon a time, a fisherman and his wife lived-in a small run-down shack on a beach near the sea. They were very poor. Early every day the fisherman went out in his little boat hoping to catch enough fish for their meal and perhaps sell some at the market.

One day the fisherman was out at sea and a great storm arose. The wind was hard; the waves were high and crashed over his little boat. He was very afraid.

Suddenly, the waves tossed a fat fish in the boat - the fisherman was happy - at last something to eat and some to sell at the market!

He grabbed the fish to put in his basket when, suddenly, it cried out, "Please, don't eat me! I'll grant you one wish if you let me live!"

Well, you can imagine the old fisherman's surprise he had a magic fish that talked! But, he was a very kind man and felt sorry for it - he let it go, and threw the fish back into the sea.

When he told his wife what happened, she was furious! "What!" she screamed! "Threw it back in the sea? You go back and find that fish and tell him you want a beautiful home with servants and carriages and lots of food!"

The next morning the fisherman set out in his boat with a heavy heart. He didn't want to take advantage of the fish. But his wife was very angry and he had to make her happy.

He rowed far out to sea, calling, "Oh, magic fish, please come!" he yelled. "My wife wants me to talk to you."

The winds started to blow the boat and the waves bounced the small craft hard up and down. Finally in the late afternoon the fish swam up and said, "I hear you, Fisherman. What is it your wife wants?"

"Oh, good fish," he started. "I am sorry to bother you. My wife wants a big home with servants and lots of food."

"Go home." said the fish. "Her wish is granted."

When the fisherman arrived home he didn't recognize his house. On the beach was a magnificent mansion with hundreds of servants walking around. Horses and carriages were lined up at the front gate while in the dining hall his wife was eating a big dinner and had many elegantly dressed people at the table.

"You fool!" She screamed at him! "You should have told the fish I want to be the king! This is not fine enough for me! Go back and tell the fish I want to be king!"

The next morning the poor fisherman left the mansion early and rowed out to sea. The winds came up and rocked the boat hard. It was dangerous - he clung to the sides of the little boat. The water was angry, the waves pounded the boat. The fisherman was afraid to call the fish, but he was more afraid of his wife.

"Oh, fish," he called. "Help me, please! My wife is very angry. Please come and hear me!"

Finally the fish appeared at the side of the boat. "Fisherman," he said. "Go home. Your wife is now the king! Do not call me again or there will be great sorrow for you." And the fish swam away with his tail slamming into the waves.

It was night time when the fisherman finally rowed home. He was very tired.

There, where his little house had been, was a huge castle with attendants dressed in blue velvet sitting in gold saddles on black horses. Soldiers dressed in fine swollen suits with gold buttons and gleaming swords at their side marched in precision to guard the doors. Servants dashed up and down the castle stairs carrying food on large silver trays to all the visitors.

There, on the throne sat his wife, dressed in red velvet and gold lace. When she saw him she threw her silver goblet at him - deep red wine like blood fell over his shabby clothes. She screamed, "You fool! This is not good enough for me! Go back to the fish and tell him I want to be God!"

The fisherman was terrified! He stared at his wife and tried to speak but the words stuck in his throat. His feet refused to move.

She screamed again, "Go! You fool! GO!"

With a heavy heart, the fisherman walked slowly to his little boat. His head hanging low; his heart beating fast.

The sky was black; huge, rolling clouds thundered with anger. Wind whipped the waves into a white froth against the small craft. The fisherman had trouble climbing into the boat but he managed to grab an oar to help him.

No sooner had the boat started for the sea when the fish swam up to the fisherman. Thunder roared, waves smashed against the boat. In a flash of lightening the fish spoke, "Fisherman, go back to your home." and disappeared into the deep water.

The fisherman fell into a deep sleep. His boat drifted all night in the water and floated to shore. At the dawn the sea was quiet.

He opened his eyes, there was his little house, the run-down shack he had before he found the magic fish.

His wife sat, crying at all that was lost.

Greed destroys all that it touches.

THE GOOSE THAT LAYS THE GOLDEN EGGS

Aesop

Once upon a time there was a farmer who had many fat geese. He was very proud of his flock and they sold well at the market. The geese were fat and laid big eggs which he also sold and made a good living.

The farmer and his wife were very happy, but the farmer would always wonder if there were a way he could make even more money and live a richer life. He wanted to be better than his neighbors, have a bigger house and bigger carriage.

The farmer had a goose boy who fed the geese, collected the eggs and made sure they were safe in their pen at night.

One bright spring day, the goose boy went to gather the eggs. There, in a big nest, were 3 gold eggs!

The goose boy stared and stared. Then, he couldn't control his excitement! He ran to the barn where the farmer was working.

"Farmer? Farmer!" the boy cried. "The goose, the goose has laid golden eggs - three of them!"

The farmer couldn't believe his ears; he put down his rake and shovel - surely the boy was seeing things!

The farmer ran up to the nest and there, big as door knobs, were three big, beautiful gold eggs! He jumped up and down for joy! He yelled and shouted, "I'm rich! Rich!"

The neighbors heard him crying out and they ran over to see what was going on. Imagine their shock when they looked in the nest and saw the golden eggs! How jealous they were!

Well, the farmer got very greedy. He sold the eggs and made so much money he wanted more, more and more! He thought, "Hmmm…there I so much gold outside the Goose - what if I killed it and took all the gold at once! I would be richer than the King!

The farmer jumped up and down for joy! "Richer than the King!" He cried!

So he killed the goose and looked and looked and looked for the gold in the goose - but there was none. It was a magic goose that could only lay the eggs - it had no gold inside of it.

Now the farmer was poor. He had no goose and no eggs. He was out of business - he had killed the goose that lays the golden eggs.

The farmer had nothing. All the neighbors called him a fool and left him alone, never to be friends again.

Greed destroys all that it touches.

ABOUT THE AUTHOR

Carolyn Franklin

M.A. Communication Studies

M. A. Education

B. A. Psychology

Opera singer, Bel Canto method

Private coach voice/speech development

Conduct Communication seminars

Conduct classes in Carl Orff Reading Readiness

Life Choices Consultant

voicedynamicscf@yahoo.com

OTHER BOOKS BY CAROLYN FRANKLIN

Adam: First Man or First Mouse?

Athena: Goddess of Communication Strategies

Attorneys: Public Speaking

Coping With Bullies: A gentle approach

E-Z Dictionary: Use the Right, Rite, Wright, Write Word

Emotional Intelligence

Just Be Yourself, Whoever That Is!

Public Speaking Made Easier

RX For Your Communication Ills

The Story of Mary: Mayhem, Mirth and Miracles

You Can Catch More Flies With Honey

Your Voice Your Personality

Women At Work: Win-Win Strategies

Women Bullying Women

www.ingramcontent.com/pod-product-compliance
Lightning Source LLC
Chambersburg PA
CBHW061809250726

48657CB00001B/364